HARTFORD

New England's Rising Star

STEVE LASCHEVER

HARTFORD

New England's Rising Star

JACK McCONNELL

Joe Zwiebel, publisher

Liz Haley Glaviano, editor and writer

Christopher Miller, art director

Lynn Mika, Profiles in Excellence designer

LEONARD HELLERMAN

GREATER HARTFORD
ARTS COUNCIL

Let's
GO!

Enjoy
Support
Arts &
Heritage

Hartford
New England's
Rising Star℠

FLETCHER
THOMPSON
ARCHITECTURE
ENGINEERING
INTERIOR DESIGN

PAUL CONEE

Outdoor musical performances are just one of the keys to the region's vitality.

© Copyright 2005 by New England Profiles and the Hartford Business Journal.
ISBN # 0-9668420-2-2
Library of Congress Card Catalogue Number: 2004115232.

All rights reserved. No part of this work may be reproduced or copied in any form
or by any means, except for brief excerpts in conjunction with book reviews,
without prior written permission of the publisher.

New England Profiles
15 Lewis Street Suite 400
Hartford, CT 06103

Publisher: Joe Zwiebel
Editor: Liz Haley Glaviano
Art Director: Christopher Miller
Project Coordinator: Kate Phelps
Profiles in Excellence Designer: Lynn Mika
Profiles in Excellence Copy Editor: Erika J. Phillips
Profiles in Excellence Writers: Cara Baruzzi, Thayer Bennett, Karen Cortés, Megan
Goold-Rindge, Laura Manente, Kate Phelps
Profiles in Excellence Sales Director: Gail Lebert
Profiles in Excellence Account Managers: Betsy Abeles Kravitz, Lydia Ashford, Diane
DeGray, Pamela Grant, David Hartley, William Lambot, Tuesday Russell, Nancy Thody
Editorial Interns: Jeffrey Wajcs and Elizabeth Pytka
Special thanks to Carol Latter and Diane Weaver Dunne for their research assistance.

Distributed by Connecticut River Press, 111 Holmes Road, Newington CT 06111
(860) 666-0615

Printed in the U.S.A. by Walsworth Publishing Company, Marceline, MO.
Dustjacket printed by Lebon Press, Hartford, CT.

OVERLEAF PHOTO: LEONARD HELLERMAN

Hartford, Connecticut's capital city, certainly is the brightest of New England's rising stars. Bursting onto the 21st century scene re-energized with a flurry of economic and cultural growth, Hartford – and the 32 towns comprising the Greater Hartford region – is in the midst of a phenomenal economic and cultural renaissance. The area quickly is developing the reputation of being *the* place to live, work, learn, visit and play.

Visions are turning into reality here, a reality being made possible by the groups, both public and private, which have invested so much in our region's future. Among the most vital are the MetroHartford Alliance and the Hartford Image Project (HIP). The Alliance, by bringing together the area's economic development leadership, has helped to create an environment that supports ambitious plans and robust execution, while HIP, a partnership of local, regional, and city organizations and businesses, has taken on the task of promoting the region through the Hartford: New England's Rising Star marketing campaign. A prime mover in these plans is the State of Connecticut, whose $750 million investment has contributed greatly to the development of the capital city's major projects and new landmarks.

The largest of these is the mixed-use development called Adriaen's Landing. This site will feature the Connecticut Convention Center and high-rise Marriott Hartford Downtown, an adjacent retail and entertainment district, and the new Connecticut Center for Science & Exploration. In addition, new and renovated hotel properties are popping up throughout the Downtown Hartford area, including the complete renovation of the 392-room Hilton Hartford. The region also boasts new and enhanced sports, arts and entertainment facilities. And with the $200 million expansion of Bradley International Airport in Windsor Locks, it is easier than ever to get here. Thanks to the new 2,300-car Morgan Street Garage, parking in Hartford is more accessible and affordable once you arrive.

KAREN O'MAXFIELD

The region's ethnic diversity is reflected in many cultural festivals, like the West Indian Independence Celebrations.

TODD MEAGHER

Our diverse, multi-cultural city's renewed vitality can be seen around every street corner, as ambitious visions turn into brick-and-mortar reality. Some $2 billion in new housing, shops, restaurants, hotels and other commercial development are soon to be seen on Hartford's horizon. The energy here is palpable, as the sounds of a region building a new reality fill the air.

Regionally, a host of other landmark developments are on the rise. From ESPN's $500 million expansion of its Bristol-based headquarters to the University of Connecticut's 21st Century UConn programs, which are part of the college's whopping $1.3 billion expansion initiative, exciting, fresh and varied projects are taking shape. The region's retail landscape is rapidly expanding as well, with the emergence of developments like Evergreen Walk in South Windsor, a 300,000-square-foot high-end lifestyle center to the Shoppes at Farmington Valley, Canton, an upscale retail center.

And although our eyes remain focused on the area's exciting future, we are reminded constantly of our Colonial past. The region, rich with enchanting parks, rural farmlands, and countless historic places, is one of breathtaking beauty, steeped in abundant history. From the Old State House in Downtown Hartford and the Noah Webster House in West Hartford to the American Clock & Watch Museum in Bristol and the Buttolph-Williams House in Wethersfield, our past is alive, and our cultural heritage continuously celebrated.

Fun for the whole family can be found throughout the area's 32 towns, in its tourist attractions. The homes of renowned authors Mark Twain and Harriet Beecher Stowe stand as proud symbols of Hartford's rich history, preserved for generations to come.

Hartford's Wadsworth Atheneum, the oldest public art museum in the country, features artwork and artifacts from around the world.

ALLEN PHILLIPS

JOHN WOLLWERTH

This celebration of culture – old and new – also is reflected in the area's performance and visual arts. It is no accident that Hartford ranks in the top 6 percent of all North American cities for its vital and abundant art scene. Support for the arts is a cornerstone of our lives in Greater Hartford, as so many of our companies – both public and private – donate proudly and generously to our many arts and cultural organizations.

The arts here flourish with a list of venerable institutions that would make any region proud. Among them are the Wadsworth Atheneum Museum of Art, the oldest public art institution in the country, which soon will be undergoing major expansions; The Bushnell Center for the Performing Arts, which features off-Broadway hits, as well as performances by the Hartford Symphony Orchestra and Connecticut Opera; the Tony Award-winning Hartford Stage; Theater Works, an intimate, off-Broadway-style theater that features contemporary plays; the CTnow.com Meadows Music Centre, that showcases live music from internationally renowned artists; and the Artists Collective, an organization that offers high-quality training in the performing arts for young people in the city's poorest neighborhoods. Art galleries, along with dance and music studios dot the region as well, and are home to numerous successful commercial and fine artists.

In the realm of commerce, the capital city and surrounding towns are home to many of America's leading corporations, including United Technologies Corporation and the Stanley Works, to name just two. The region also boasts some of the finest hospitals in our country. Among the standouts are Saint Francis Hospital and Medical Center, The Connecticut Children's Medical Center and, of course, Hartford Hospital.

JOHN MULDOON

The Buttolph-Williams House in Wethersfield, dating from circa 1710 to 1720, is considered to be the best-restored house of this period in the Connecticut River Valley.

STEVE LASCHEVER

There is no shortage of skilled and motivated talent to fill the positions at these institutions. From Capital Community College's new 304,000-square-foot campus in Downtown Hartford and the University of Hartford's $67-million expansion and redevelopment project, to the University of Connecticut, also undergoing a massive expansion, and the esteemed Trinity College, young people here don't have to look very far to obtain a superior education. The University of Connecticut Business School in Downtown Hartford is a cutting-edge learning center for the area's business professionals, giving them the competitive advantage needed to succeed in today's business world.

If it's housing students and young professionals are looking for, the region has an abundance, with more on the way. A number of private developers in partnership with the City of Hartford, the State of Connecticut and economic development organizations are contributing to revitalizing the city with more than 1,000 new residential units.

In Hartford's neighborhoods, housing revitalization is in full swing, as home owners and tenants alike are actively preserving and honoring the fine and unique structures of Hartford's past. Our neighborhoods and towns are rich in ethnic tradition and culturally alive. In many, residents merely need to walk down the street or around the block to sample some of the finest ethnic cuisine New England has to offer.

JACK McCONNELL

Bushnell Park in Hartford hosts a variety of performances throughout the summer months. It was the country's first municipal park to be conceived, built and paid for by citizens through a popular vote.

George Tuffin recreates the feeling of an old-fashioned general store at the Salmon Brook Historical Society in Granby.

HUNTER NEAL

hether it's enjoying a cappuccino at Mozzicato DePasquale Bakery & Pastry Shop in Hartford's "Little Italy" neighborhood, or sampling traditional German cuisine at the East Side Restaurant in Downtown New Britain, the region offers countless cultural delights. After grabbing a quick bite to eat, visitors and locals alike find the nightlife vibrant and easily accessible. Area bars and clubs liven up the evenings, offering live performances in Jazz, Blues, Rock n' roll, Reggae, Hip-Hop and Country.

If the club scene is not for you, there also are a variety of sports venues and options in the region. The Hartford Wolf Pack hockey team and UConn men's and women's championship basketball games at the Hartford Civic Center offer excitement, as do the University of Connecticut's division A football games at Rentschler Field, a new world-class sports and entertainment stadium, located in East Hartford.

Here at home in this charming and historically rich New England setting, Hartford hustles and bustles with the verve and pulse of a large city, minutes from rural beauty and a slower pace. It truly offers the best of all worlds.

History, vitality, energy and diversity – it's all here. This is Greater Hartford's story.

– Liz Haley Glaviano

JOHN MULDOON

The Greater Hartford region offers a diversity of landscapes, from urban to suburban to rural farmlands.

JACK MCCONNELL

STEVE LASCHEVER

LYNN MIKA

Downtown Hartford's lunchtime crowd outside of State House Square.

A statue honouring Hartford dentist Horace Wells, who discovered modern anesthesia, is on display in Bushnell Park.

JACK McCONNELL

LEONARD HELLERMAN

LEONARD HELLERMAN

Abstract reflections at Union Station in Downtown Hartford.

JACK McCONNELL

Reflections at State House Square.

LANNY NAGLER

LEONARD HELLERMAN

(Top) The Old State House in Downtown Hartford, built in 1796, is the oldest statehouse in the country.

(Left) In October 1826, the State of Connecticut contracted John Stanwood to build a cupola on the Old State House. Topped with a statue of Justice, the cupola was finished in 1827.

(Right) Today, the Old State House is designated a National Historic Landmark by the U.S. Department of the Interior and serves as a museum.

JACK McCONNELL

LEONARD HELLERMAN

LEONARD HELLERMAN

Hartford's State Capitol, located at the edge of Bushnell Park, is not only the seat of state government but also serves as a significant tourist draw.

LEONARD HELLERMAN

LEONARD HELLERMAN

(Left and top) Hartford's City Hall, listed on the National Register of Historic Places, was designed in the Beaux-Arts style (then called Georgian). This majestic landmark opened in 1915.

(Right) Community organizer Eddie Perez was elected Hartford's first Hispanic mayor Nov. 6, 2001. During his second term, beginning in January 2004, Perez became the full-time "CEO" of the city under charter revisions approved by voters.

Connecticut Convention Center

"Largest
Event Space in
Southern
New England"

Exhibit, Ballroom
and
Meeting Rooms
Totaling 550,000
Square Feet

860-728-6789
www.hartford.com

State of Connecticut, John G. Rowland, Governor
City of Hartford, Eddie Perez, Mayor
Waterford Development, LLC

Hartford
New England's
Rising Star™

STEVE LASCHEVER

When construction is completed, Downtown Hartford's Adriaen's Landing project will boast The Connecticut Convention Center, the Marriott Hartford Downtown, street-level shops, and the hands-on Connecticut Center for Science & Exploration.

LEONARD HELLERMAN

STEVE LASCHEVER

Intimate outdoor concerts liven up the summer nights.

LEONARD HELLERMAN

STEVE LASCHEVER

(Top left) The Phoenix Gateway is a pedestrian walkway that connects Constitution Plaza to Riverfront Plaza.

(Top right) The Phoenix Building, a 14-story glass and steel high rise, is commonly referred to as the "Boat Building." It was constructed in 1964 and is considered one of the city's modern landmarks.

(Right) Constitution Plaza, constructed during the early 1960s as part of an urban renewal project, is the site of numerous festivals.

STEVE LASCHEVER

LEONARD HELLERMAN

Downtown Hartford's landscape is an interesting juxtaposition of historic and modern buildings.

LYNN MIKA

This lamppost serves as a decorative accent on the gates that enter into the State House Square courtyard.

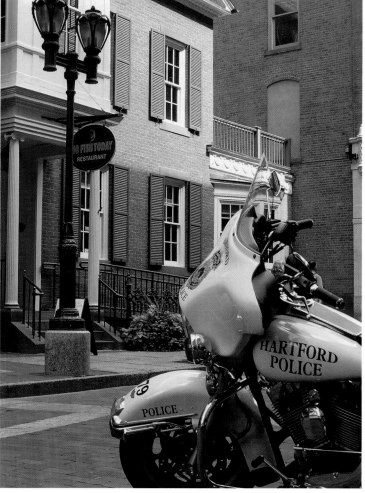

LYNN MIKA

Downtown Hartford's Pratt Street.

The Soldiers and Sailors Memorial Arch was designed by city architect George Keller, whose other works include the Charter Oak Cultural Center and Park Terrace Row Houses. In 1886, this brownstone arch was dedicated to the 4,000 Hartford citizens who served in the Civil War, as well as the 400 who died for the Union.

LYNN MIKA

STEVE LASCHEVER

(Above) The plaza outside the Old State House is a favorite spot for city workers to take a stroll and pick up some fresh flowers on their lunch hour.

(Right) Puritan clergyman Thomas Hooker, born in 1586, is credited with being the founder of Hartford. A native of England, he immigrated to Massachusetts, and later moved with many of his congregation to Hartford, where he served as pastor until his death in 1647. He was considered by many to be a leader in both religious and governmental arenas.

JACK McCONNELL

VINCENT SALVATORE

The Corning Fountain in Bushnell Park, erected in 1899, is a 30-foot tall monument fashioned out of stone and marble. It showcases dynamic sculptures of the city's first inhabitants, the Saukiog Indians.

This sculpture depicts Hartford native Samuel Colt with a factory worker from his Colt Firearms plant, located beside the Connecticut River in Hartford. Colt became famous the world over for his Colt revolvers.

JACK McCONNELL

STEVE LASCHEVER

This bronze statue of Connecticut-born Revolutionary War patriot Nathan Hale is located on Main Street outside the Wadsworth Atheneum.

Detail of frieze work, Soldiers and Sailors Memorial Arch.

STEVE LASCHEVER

STEVE LASCHEVER

STEVE LASCHEVER

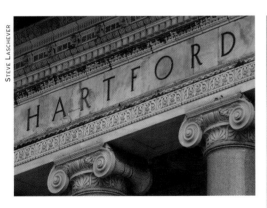

STEVE LASCHEVER

STEVE LASCHEVER

Sculptural details found
around Hartford.
At top right,
Alexander Caulder's
"Stegosaurus" sculpture
stands proudly outside
the Wadsworth
Atheneum.

PAUL CONE

STEVE LASCHEVER

STEVE LASCHEVER

Hartford's
monuments
and skyline
provide
the backdrop
for a region
in motion.

One Financial Plaza, better known as the "Gold Building" in Downtown Hartford at dusk.

CityPlace 1 at night.

VINCENT SALVATORE

The 1950s-era Olympia Diner in Newington.

STEVE LASCHEVER

Lena's First & Last Pizzaria in Hartford serves up some of the area's best pizza and homemade soups.

JOHN MULDOON

JOHN MULDOON

Quality nightlife and dining options abound in Greater Hartford.

JOHN MULDOON

JOHN MULDOON

STEVE LASCHEVER

West Hartford Center, an upscale shopping and dining destination, is one of the area's most popular gathering spots, and a model for other town centers. West Hartford Center will soon be expanded with the addition of Blue Back Square, a $158.8 million mixed-use development, featuring shops, condominiums, offices and a movie theatre.

JOHN MULDOON

The Monday Night Jazz Series, held in Bushnell Park, is one of the region's many cultural highlights.

JOHN MULDOON

Guitar Under the Stars, held at the riverfront in Downtown Hartford, is headed by internationally renowned guitarist Daniel Salazar Jr., center. Guitarists, from left, Lorena Garay, and Daniel Salazar III, are members of his performance group.

STEVE LASCHEVER

STEVE LASCHEVER

STEVE LASCHEVER

The Hartford Symphony
Orchestra, under Music Director
Edward Cumming, left, performs
live symphonic music throughout
Greater Hartford and is regarded
as one of the country's leading
regional orchestras.

T. CHARLES ERICKSON

Mary Zimmerman's Broadway smash "Metamorphoses" found a home at the Hartford Stage in 2004, where it played to a packed house in an extended engagement. The production featured a 30-foot pool of water that dominated Hartford Stage's thrust stage. Pictured are Erika LaVonn, foreground, and Anne Fogarty.

JENNIFER LESTER

"Madama Butterfly" as performed by the Connecticut Opera, the sixth-oldest professional opera company in the country.

JENNIFER LESTER

The ghost of Jacob Marley (Noble Shropshire) recounts his ultimate fate of eternal woe in Dickens' "A Christmas Carol — A Ghost Story of Christmas," adapted and directed by Michael Wilson at the Hartford Stage.

FIRST NATIONAL TOURING COMPANY OF THE PRODUCERS THE NEW MEL BROOKS MUSICAL/PAUL KOLNIK

A scene from the Tony Award-winning hit "The Producers" held at The Bushnell Center for the Performing Arts.

PAUL KOLNIK

"Hairspray" made its Connecticut premiere at The Bushnell in September 2003.

JENNIFER LESTER

"Salome" as performed by the Connecticut Opera.

THOMAS GIROIR

Hartt bachelor of fine arts dance majors, Antonio Lytle and Jenrett Doucett, at a dance performance at The Hartt School of the University of Hartford. The Hartt School offers undergraduate programs in music, dance and theatre.

LANNY NAGLER

A scene from "10 Unknowns" at Theater Works in Downtown Hartford. This venue features contemporary plays in an intimate, off-Broadway-style setting.

WAYNE DOMBKOWSKI

Richard Sugarman, founding president of the Connecticut Forum, with Bill Russell, at the "Being Black" forum. The Connecticut Forum presents four issue-focused forums each season, featuring celebrity and renowned panelists, at The Bushnell.

WAYNE DOMBKOWSKI

The "Behind the Scenes with the Simpsons" forum, May 2004.

JACK McCONNELL

Established in 1916, the Durham Fair is the largest agricultural fair in Connecticut.
It is traditionally held the last full weekend of September, and features various agricultural programs,
livestock exhibits, baking contests, and other family-fun activities.

JOHN MULDOON

The region's music scene includes numerous Jazz events, including the Greater Hartford Festival of Jazz.

RIVERFRONT RECAPTURE

A night of music on the riverfront in Downtown Hartford.

JOHN MULDOON

Dancing the night away at the Moodus Jazz Festival.

JOHN MULDOON

STEVE LASCHEVER

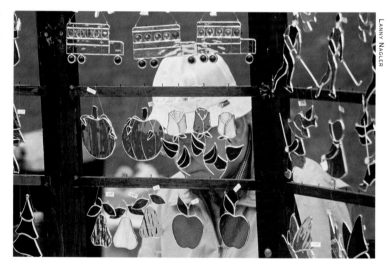
LANNY NAGLER

From town festivals and cow
parades to ethnic celebrations,
and agricultural and craft fairs,
the region offers year-round,
exciting, family-fun
entertainment options.

PETER GLASS

PETER GLASS

PETER GLASS

JOHN MULDOON

PAUL CONEE

PAUL CONEE

PAUL CONEE

PAUL CONEE

PAUL CONEE

The past comes alive with historical re-enactments and fife and drum corps performances held in several towns throughout the region.

JOHN MULDOON

RIVERFRONT RECAPTURE

(Left) Among the celebrations at many Native American powwows are drumming group and dancing competitions.

(Above) Freedom Schooner Amistad provides an opportunity for both residents and tourists to reconnect to the historical roots Hartford shares with the Amistad Incident of 1839. It also serves as an icon and catalyst for teaching the historic lessons inherent in the Amistad Incident.

John Muldoon

John Muldoon

John Muldoon

JOHN MULDOON

LANNY NAGLER

The Farmington
Antiques Weekend,
held each year at the
Farmington Polo
Grounds, features
the merchandise of
several hundred
international antique
dealers.

JOHN MULDOON

From Connecticut's beaches to its rural farms, the state's diverse landscapes offer an assortment of activities for children and adults alike.

JACK McCONNELL

JACK McCONNELL

JOHN MULDOON

Jet skiing at the Connecticut shore.

JACK McCONNELL

Kayaking on the Farmington River.

RIVERFRONT RECAPTURE

Rowing on the Connecticut River. Riverfront Recapture's reconnection of Metro Hartford to the Connecticut River was instrumental in helping the city define its future. Now a bustling sports and cultural center, the riverfront also features a two-story Victorian style boathouse in Riverside Park, which provides space for the popular community rowing program to expand.

RIVERFRONT RECAPTURE

The new park system created in Hartford along the Connecticut River by Riverfront Recapture serves as a venue for numerous recreational and sporting opportunities, including the Capitol City Triathlon.

JOHN MULDOON

LANNY NAGLER

(Above) Fly fishing is a popular regional pastime.

(Right) Tubing down the Farmington River.

Hunter Neal

Jack McConnell

In every season, the region's diverse landscape allows for a variety of sporting options.

Hunter Neal

Lanny Nagler

Golfing options abound in the region, which features numerous public and private courses.

Fox hunt in Simsbury.

The Ebony Horsewomen is a community service organization, developed and
directed by African-American female equestrians.
Its mission is to encourage and empower inner-city youth to live successful
lives, through the use of horses.

PAUL CONEE

The Hartford Vintage Baseball Invitational is held each 4rth of July weekend in Bushnell Park. The Hartford Senators Base Ball Club is a vintage team modeled after the Hartford-based minor league team of the early 1920s.

JERRY MARGOLIS

GSPETRO/PIXGSP.COM

(Left) The University of Connecticut's Huskies football team got a huge boost in 2003 with the completion of Rentschler Field, its new home base in East Hartford. Rentschler is the newest and most modern college football stadium in the country.

(Above) The New Britain Rock Cats are the Double A affiliate of the 2004 American League Central Division Champions. The Rock Cats play their home games at New Britain Stadium. Shown is former Rock Cats outfielder and "Minnesota Twins Top Prospect," Jason Kubel.

DEREK DUDEK

Each October, thousands of runners participate in the Greater Hartford Marathon. The race course, which begins and ends in Bushnell Park, combines the vibrancy of Downtown Hartford with brilliant autumn foliage and country roads along the Connecticut River, and with lively streets in the city's West End.

STAFFORD MOTOR SPEEDWAY

CHRIS RUTSCH

(Above) The Stafford Motor Speedway, a 100-acre motor sport racing facility, opened in 1870 as the Stafford Springs Agricultural Park, and was later converted into a half-mile racing track that has been home to weekly NASCAR races for more than 40 years.

(Right) The Hartford Wolf Pack plays an American Hockey League schedule from October to April at the Hartford Civic Center Veterans Memorial Coliseum. The multi-national squad includes players from Canada, Latvia, Sweden, Russia, Slovakia and the Czech Republic.

JERRY MARGOLIS

JERRY MARGOLIS

JERRY MARGOLIS

Taliek Brown was the only player in UConn history to record double-figure assists in consecutive Big East regular season games.

UConn men's basketball coach Jim Calhoun.

UConn women's basketball coach Geno Auriemma.

JERRY MARGOLIS

LANNY NAGLER

The University of Connecticut became the "Home of Champions" in April 2004, when UConn won NCAA championships in both men's and women's basketball on two consecutive days. UConn was the first Division I school to win both titles in the same year. In the past few years, UConn has won several NCAA Championships, including 1999 men's basketball, 2000 women's basketball, 2000 men's soccer, 2002 and 2003 women's basketball, and 2004 men's and women's basketball.

Diana Taurasi was a key player in the UConn women's basketball NCAA championship victory in April 2004.

JERRY MARGOLIS

(Above) Rentschler Field, part of the state's effort to revitalize the Hartford area and elevate the University of Connecticut's football program to national status, opened in East Hartford July 29, 2003.

(Right) Anna Kournikova, who plays for the Kansas City Explorers, in her match against the Hartford FoxForce, Summer 2004. The FoxForce is a World Team Tennis franchise.

(Far right) Mardy Fish, ranked 30th in the world, was drafted by the FoxForce in April 2004 and has played two matches for the FoxForce at the Apple Arena at Blue Fox Run Golf Course. Fish also is a member of the 2005 Davis Cup team. FoxForce will be returning for its sixth year in July 2005 at the Apple Arena.

HARTFORD FOXFORCE

HARTFORD FOXFORCE

PAUL CONEE

LANNY NAGLER

STEVE LASCHEVER

Lisa Farrell, owner of Full Blooms Florist, outside her shop in Hartford.

HUNTER NEAL

John Marona, of Quiet Sports in Collinsville, ties a line.

STEVE LASCHEVER

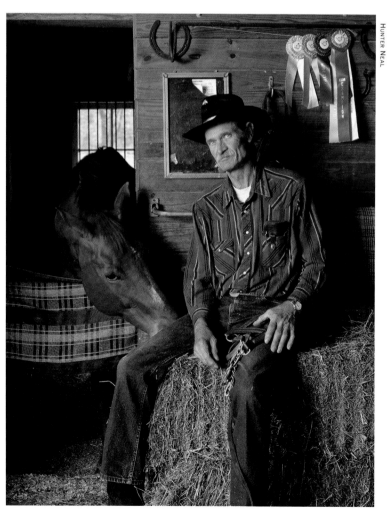

HUNTER NEAL

(Above) Sisters Monica
Ross, left, Hortense Ross,
and Precious Ross-Ellis
(not pictured) run Medical
Temp Force on Albany
Avenue. Their purchase and
renovation of the building
housing their business
demonstrates the
commitment each has to
the neighbourhood.

(Left) Vince Bishop
of Folly Farm in Weatogue.

NICK LACY

Janice Bennett weaves a very old craft at her Farmington Valley Arts Center studio.

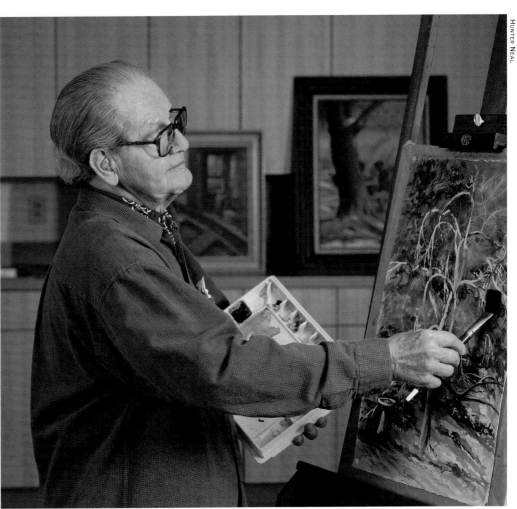

HUNTER NEAL

Bob Francis, a resident of Seabury Retirement Community, has been a professional artist his entire life.

CARMINE FILLORAMO

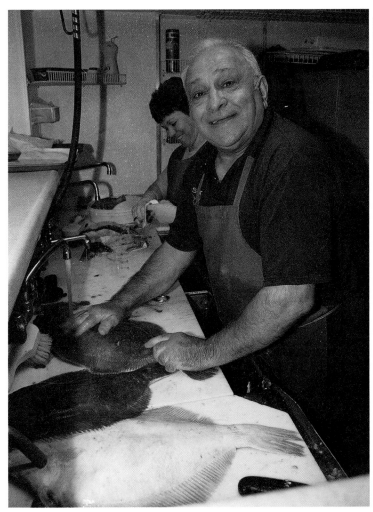

Constantino da Branca preparing fish Portuguese style at Solmar Fish Market on Park Street in Hartford.

Hartford police officer Maurice Washington on duty in Downtown Hartford.

Scott's Jamaican Bakery store manager Clarence Solomon, left, with store owner, George Scott, inside his Albany Avenue store.

Alfresco dining in West Hartford Center.

LUIS VALENTIN

Hispanic culture is thriving in the Greater Hartford area.

LUIS VALENTIN

STEVE LASCHEVER

Gino Mozzicato and his son Rino decorate dozens of tiered wedding cakes each week at their bakery on Franklin Avenue, Mozzicato DePasquale Bakery & Pastry Shop. Franklin Avenue is also known as "Little Italy."

STEVE LASCHEVER

Casa Lisboa in Hartford has been dishing up Portuguese food for more than 30 years.

HUNTER NEAL

Dick Portfolio roasting
beans in his German
Probat coffee roaster at
the Coffee Trade in Avon.

STEVE LASCHEVER

STEVE LASCHEVER

The periphery of Bushnell Park is home to a variety of ethnic food vendors who serve the city's lunchtime crowd.

STEVE LASCHEVER

Preparing
Eastern delights
at the
A Dong Market in
West Hartford.

JOHN MULDOON

STEVE LASCHEVER

Greater Hartford is home to a dynamic mix of ethnic cuisines and specialty food shops, including Afghan, Indian and Asian.

STEVE LASCHEVER

STEVE LASCHEVER

LANNY NAGLER

Firefighters protect lives and property throughout the Greater Hartford region.

LEONARD HELLERMAN

Ray Dunaway and Diane Smith of WTIC NewsTalk 1080's "Mornings with Ray & Diane" show.

LEONARD HELLERMAN

Construction workers on Lewis Street in Downtown Hartford.

The Artists Collective on Albany Avenue in Hartford was founded by world-renowned alto saxophonist and educator Jackie McLean, and his wife Dollie, an actress, dancer and administrator, to offer high-quality training in the performing arts for young people in the city's poorest neighborhoods. Special performances by jazz greats, emerging musicians, and nationally recognized dance and theatre companies also give residents of the Greater Hartford region a unique opportunity to learn about and enjoy the arts and cultural traditions of people of African descent. Featured are Dollie McLean, center, and Master Choreographer Lee "Aca" Thompson.

Middletown resident Willie J. Nelson performs for the theatre-going crowd outside The Bushnell Center for the Performing Arts.

STEVE LASCHEVER

Maurice Mathis, owner of Moe's Furniture, in Hartford.

KAREN O'MAXFIELD

STEVE LASCHEVER

Margaret Merriman, director of the Parkville Senior Citizen's Center for the past 30 years, is shown here with the Memory Quilt. This quilt was created by neighbourhood seniors in conjunction with a grant from Real Art Ways.

Customers at Leaves and Pages bookstore in New Britain.

JOHN MULDOON

Showing off tattoo art on Park Street in Hartford.

LEONARD HELLERMAN

A scene from Union Station in Downtown Hartford. Union Station is the city's rail and bus transportation hub.

KAREN O'MAXFIELD

Giselda Sarmiento at the Hooker Day Parade in Hartford.

KAREN O'MAXFIELD

Saluting the Vietnam Memorial in Hartford's Southwest Neighbourhood.

STEVE LASCHEVER

Private 1st Class Nicholas Uccello, a military police officer serving in the Connecticut National Guard, kept watch over Bradley International Airport, post 9/11.

JACK MCCONNELL

The Connecticut Firemen's Historical Society in Manchester is located in a turn-of-the-century firehouse which features hand and horse-pulled firefighting equipment, including an 1860 steam fire engine and antique firefighting items.

STEVE LASCHEVER

Joshua Holtzberg at a rehearsal for his Bar Mitzvah.

STEVE LASCHEVER

The Glaviano Wedding, Spring 2004.

JACK MCCONNELL

Our regional churches and collective places of worship display magnificent stained glass windows and a variety of sculptures. Shown above is the interior of Trinity Methodist Church in New Britain.

First Church of Christ's spire in Old Wethersfield. The church is an historic landmark, dating back to 1761.

PAUL CONEE

The Cathedral of Saint Joseph in Hartford offers impressive examples of religious art in several mediums, including mosaics, stained glass, and sculpture in both metal and stone.

JOHN MULDOON

JACK McCONNELL

(Above) Holy Trinity Orthodox Church in New Britain.

(Right) Center Church in Hartford has one of the most beautiful steeples in the region. The 185-foot-high structure is floodlit in perpetual memory of loved ones through contributions to the Let There Be Light Memorial Fund.

JACK MCCONNELL

The following
pages offer a
glimpse into the
region's
breathtaking
scenery.

JACK MCCONNELL

JOHN MULDOON

JACK MCCONNELL

JACK MCCONNELL

LEONARD HELLERMAN

LEONARD HELLERMAN

VINCENT SALVATORE

JACK MCCONNELL

JACK McCONNELL

JACK McCONNELL

JACK McCONNELL

JACK McCONNELL

JOHN MULDOON

JACK McCONNELL

JACK McCONNELL

JACK MCCONNELL

STEVE LASCHEVER

HUNTER NEAL

JACK MCCONNELL

JACK McCONNELL

HUNTER NEAL

LEONARD HELLERMAN

JACK McCONNELL

LEONARD HELLERMAN

LEONARD HELLERMAN

LEONARD HELLERMAN

JACK McCONNELL

Cedar Hill Cemetery in Hartford is the final resting place of many famous persons, including Samuel Colt, Horace Wells, J.P. Morgan, Thomas Gallaudet and Wallace Stevens.

The Ancient Burying Ground in Downtown Hartford houses approximately 6,000 graves, some dating as far back as the 17th century. It is believed, (though not proven) that the remains of Thomas Hooker lie here.

JACK McCONNELL

Leonard Hellerman

Tobacco farmers in Windsor. In 1640, the town's first tobacco crop was planted, with seeds brought to Connecticut from the Virginia plantations. Today, several hundred acres are still cultivated.

Jack McConnell

Steve Laschever

Windsor's town green. Windsor is known as Connecticut's first community and was founded in 1633 by settlers from Plymouth Colony in Massachusetts.

Castle Craig, located in Meriden's Hubbard Park, is a stone observation tower.

JACK McCONNELL

Built in 1876, the Goodspeed Opera House in East Haddam is dedicated to preserving America's musical theatre heritage.

JACK McCONNELL

PAUL CONEE

Elizabeth Park is the nation's oldest municipal rose garden and features more than 15,000 rose bushes and arches.

JACK MCCONNELL

The Mark Twain House & Museum is one of the region's most popular tourist attractions. Once the home of world-renowned author Samuel Clemens (who wrote under the pen name Mark Twain), it was here that many of his classics, including "The Adventures of Huckleberry Finn," were written. Twain's Hartford home is a 19-room mansion that was decorated by Louis Comfort Tiffany. It is now listed as a National Historic Landmark.

JACK MCCONNELL

LEONARD HELLERMAN

LEONARD HELLERMAN

Harriet Beecher Stowe, author of "Uncle Tom's Cabin," was born in Litchfield, Connecticut, and later worked as a teacher in Hartford. A writer for 51 years, she and her husband lived in Ohio, Maine and Massachusetts, but returned to Hartford upon his retirement. In 1873, she moved to her last home, a brick Victorian house on Forest Street, next door to Mark Twain's residence. Today, the Harriet Beecher Stowe House is open to the public, and attracts thousands of visitors each year.

LEONARD HELLERMAN

JACK McCONNELL

The Stowe Center Library & Museum in Hartford was established by Katherine Seymour Day, the grandniece of Harriet Beecher Stowe. The library has expanded from Day's collection of books, manuscripts and artifacts to a wealth of material on 19th century Americana. Today, it includes more than 12,000 books, including first editions of Beecher Stowe's works.

JACK MCCONNELL

The Noah Webster House in West Hartford is the birthplace of Noah Webster, author of the first American dictionary. It now serves as a hands-on historic site and museum.

JACK MCCONNELL

Gillette Castle State Park in East Haddam, once the home of stage actor William Gillette, is reminiscent of a medieval castle.

JOHN MULDOON

(Above) The Hill-Stead Museum, located on a 152-acre hilltop in Farmington, is a National Historic Landmark that features rare Impressionist paintings, Chinese porcelains, Japanese woodblock prints, decorative art and original furnishings.

(Right) The Museum of Connecticut History is located in the State Library and Supreme Court Building in Hartford. On permanent display are portraits of Connecticut governors, as well as historic documents, including the State's original 1662 Royal Charter, the 1639 Fundamental Orders, and the 1818 and 1964 State Constitutions.

JACK MCCONNELL

JACK MCCONNELL

The Wadsworth Atheneum displays a world-renowned collection that spans 5,000 years. Included in the museum's extensive and varied catalogue are Hudson River School landscapes, works by the Old Masters, French and American Impressionist paintings, and modernist and contemporary works. Meissen and Sevres porcelains, costumes and textiles, American furniture and decorative arts from the Pilgrim Century through the Gilded Age are among the Wadsworth's other treasures.

ALLEN PHILLIPS

ALLEN PHILLIPS

JACK MCCONNELL

JACK MCCONNELL

The University of Hartford's Museum of American Political Life features one of the nation's largest presidential campaign memorabilia collections. The museum's collections are now housed in the university's Mortensen Library, and several of its items are exhibited on both the local and national levels.

JACK MCCONNELL

A still from the Vintage Radio and Communications Museum in Windsor. This museum is dedicated to preserving the history of communications.

JACK MCCONNELL

JACK MCCONNELL

The American Silver Museum in Meriden presents the history, art and science of silver and silvermaking in the U.S. since Colonial times.

The region has a rich Native American history. Shown is a sampling of Native American artifacts from the Wood Memorial Library in South Windsor.

FOXWOODS RESORT CASINO

Schemitzun, the annual feast of Green Corn and Dance, is presented by the Mashantucket Pequot Tribal Nation. At this event, dancers and singers from around the country and Canada compete for more than $400,000 in prizes.

Foxwoods Resort Casino and Mohegan Sun Resort Casino are two of the state's largest tourist attractions.

FOXWOODS RESORT CASINO

DINOSAUR STATE PARK

DINOSAUR STATE PARK

JOHN MULDOON

(Top left) Dinosaur State Park in Rocky Hill houses 500 dinosaur tracks and related interactive exhibits.

(Top right) Edward McCarthy found the first dinosaur track while working on a construction project planned for this site. Soon after, it was determined that this area was the largest dinosaur trackway site in North America.

(Left) The American Clock & Watch Museum in Bristol houses one of the finest collections of American-made clocks on public display, featuring more than 1,500 rare clocks and watches.

STEVE LASCHEVER

The historic Bushnell Park Carousel in Hartford, located in Bushnell Park, was created circa 1914 by Solomon Stein and Harry Goldstein, the owners of Brooklyn, New York-based Artistic Carousel Company. These unique hand-carved horses truly are one of the city's gems.

LANNY NAGLER

MYSTIC AQUARIUM INSTITUTE FOR EXPLORATION

Founded in 1929, Mystic Seaport is a maritime museum, offering its visitors a well-rounded glimpse into our seafaring history.

The Mystic Aquarium Institute for Exploration is one of the state's largest tourist attractions. Its mission is to inspire people everywhere to protect our oceans by preserving their biological, ecological and cultural treasures.

JERRY MARGOLIS

Rentschler Field in East Hartford celebrated its grand opening with a performance by contemporary music legend Bruce Springsteen.

JERRY MARGOLIS

JERRY MARGOLIS

(Far left) Steven Tyler, veteran front man for Aerosmith, at the CTnow.com Meadows Music Centre, a concert venue in Hartford's North Meadows neighbourhood.

(Left) Country singer Tim McGraw at the CTnow.com Meadows Music Centre.

CONNECTICUT DEPARTMENT OF TRANSPORTATION

An aerial view of Bradley International Airport in Windsor Locks. Bradley is New England's second-largest airport and one of the fastest-growing airports in the nation.

LEONARD HELLERMAN

A Boeing B-29 is among the many aircraft and engines on display at the New England Air Museum in Windsor Locks.

JACK McCONNELL

Aerial view of Trinity College in Hartford.

SAINT JOSEPH COLLEGE

STEVE LASCHEVER

Shyamala Raman lecturing at Saint Joseph College in West Hartford.

University of Hartford winter graduates.

LEONARD HELLERMAN

Students walking across the quad at Loomis-Chaffee, a private co-educational school in Windsor. This 300-acre campus is located in Windsor at the site where it was founded in 1874.

Students at The Learning Corridor in Hartford study an impressive variety of dance techniques, including ballet, Flamenco and tap. The Learning Corridor is a public/private collaborative effort located on a 16-acre campus that houses four public magnet schools.

THE LEARNING CORRIDOR

UCONN HEALTH CENTER

An aerial view of the UConn Health Center in Farmington.

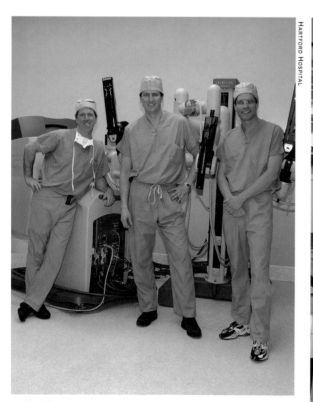

HARTFORD HOSPITAL

Hartford Hospital's surgery team in front of da Vinci. The da Vinci Surgical System was the first operative surgical robot deemed safe and effective for performing surgery by the Food and Drug Administration. From left are: Dr. Joseph Wagner, Dr. Steven Shichman and Dr. Vincent Laudone.

SAINT FRANCIS HOSPITAL AND MEDICAL CENTER

The Patient Care Tower at Saint Francis Hospital and Medical Center in Hartford was completed in 1996.

STEVE LASCHEVER

Stephen Giarratana/QualityPhotograph.com

STEVE LASCHEVER

PROFILES IN EXCELLENCE

A sampling of the dynamic and vital business enterprises, professional service firms and institutions which bring economic prosperity as well as civic, social and human connections to our region.

Each organization has a story to tell, and it is here that they are told — in their own words. Arranged by their respective year of founding, these stories chronicle the strong commitment business and industry has exhibited — and continues to contribute — toward the well-being and quality of life in Greater Hartford.

STEVE LASCHEVER

1817–1975

AMERICAN SCHOOL FOR THE DEAF

The oldest school for the deaf in the Americas was founded in Hartford in 1817. To this day, American School for the Deaf remains a tribute to the open-minded, forward-thinking citizens, both in business and government, who made it possible. It is truly a legacy of opportunity.

FEMALE STUDENTS AND FACULTY POSING IN FRONT OF THE "OLD HARTFORD" SCHOOL ON ASYLUM AVENUE AROUND 1895. THE SITE IS NOW THE HOME TO THE HARTFORD INSURANCE COMPANY.

*I*n the early 1800s, Dr. Mason Fitch Cogswell was a prominent, well-respected physician in the close-knit city of Hartford. Cogswell's daughter Alice lost her hearing from disease when she was two years old. He tried to teach her through various means, but had little success until a neighbor, Thomas H. Gallaudet, demonstrated an unusual talent in teaching the child. Cogswell then asked his friends, who included many of the most influential citizens of Hartford, to contribute funds to send Gallaudet to Europe to learn the methods of instructing deaf children that were in use there.

Upon arriving in France in 1815, Gallaudet visited the school for the deaf in Paris, the world's first such institution. He was instructed by the Abbe Sicard, its director, and his deaf assistant, Laurent Clerc. Clerc agreed to accompany Gallaudet to America and was instrumental in developing the Hartford school, the first special education facility in America.

"Public-private partnership," a popular idea in modern times, is really not so new. When Gallaudet, Clerc and Cogswell started raising funds, they fully embraced the concept. Among early private supporters of their efforts are names still remembered in the area – Charles Sigourney, Daniel Wadsworth, Timothy Dwight, Nathaniel Terry, Christopher Colt (whose son, Sam, would later found the Colt Firearms Manufacturing Co.) and others.

At the same time, organizers approached state government officials. When the Connecticut General Assembly incorporated the institution in 1816 and donated $5,000 toward its founding, it was the first state aid given to special education in the history of the United States.

The school opened April 15, 1817, on Main Street in Hartford with seven pupils, including Alice Cogswell.

Word of this new school in Hartford reached representatives in Congress, who in 1819, appropriated 23,000 acres of public domain in the territory of Alabama for the school's use. Funds from the sale of this land enabled the new school to purchase a site and erect a permanent building on Asylum Hill, where the school operated for 100 years, from 1821-1921. The public-private partnership lives on today, as the school continues to depend on a combination of private philanthropy and governmental support to fulfill its mission.

Much of the success of the institution was due to the work of its three co-founders – Cogswell, who helped secure public and legislative support and funding, and organized the governing board; Gallaudet, who was a teacher and the first headmaster; and Clerc, the first deaf teacher in America, who implemented the instructional program and facilitated the development and growth of

American Sign Language. Clerc dedicated the remainder of his life to deaf education and, through numerous contacts, brought the work of the school to the public's attention.

To address the need for a more modern facility and to accommodate anticipated growth, the school moved to its current campus at 139 N. Main St. in West Hartford, in 1921.

In fall 2001, the American School for the Deaf again made history when Dr. Harvey J. Corson became the school's first deaf executive director.

Today, more than 300 faculty and staff provide instruction and services to more than 400 full-time preschool through high school students in center-based and community-based programs; 100 adults in a variety of vocational and life-skills programs; and 50 families of deaf and hard of hearing infants and children from birth to age three. The campus includes complete facilities for all activities, including student life, work experience programs, athletics and recreation.

In addition to the education programs in West Hartford, the school offers a comprehensive range of outreach and support services for deaf and hard of hearing students and their families, regardless of placement, in partnership with local school districts.

The school maintains two regional offices, one in Norwich and the other in

Bridgeport. Services provided include early childhood support, educational and psychological assessments, counseling, audiology, cochlear implant support, sign language instruction, educational and technical assistance, and adult vocational services.

Modern technology – including high-speed Internet access, specialized computer programs and video teleconferencing – is used to enhance programming, instruction and communication.

The American School for the Deaf, a pioneer in the education of deaf and hard of hearing individuals, remains at the forefront of its field after 187 years.

A STATUE OF THOMAS H. GALLAUDET AND ALICE COGSWELL GRACES THE FRONT OF THE SCHOOL'S MAIN BUILDING ON NORTH MAIN STREET IN WEST HARTFORD.

THE SCHOOL PROVIDES INSTRUCTION AND SUPPORT SERVICES TO STUDENTS, BEGINNING AT THE PRESCHOOL LEVEL, AND ASSISTS FAMILIES OF YOUNGER CHILDREN.

TRINITY COLLEGE

Trinity College is a community united in a quest to foster critical thinking and prepare students to lead examined lives that are personally satisfying, civically responsible and socially useful.

ABOVE: ALONG THE LONG WALK ON CAMPUS.

AT RIGHT: THE DOWNES MEMORIAL CLOCK TOWER ON CAMPUS.

Trinity College was only the second college in Connecticut when it was founded by Episcopalian ministers in the spring of 1823 as Washington College (the name was changed in 1845). When the inaugural semester got under way the following fall, classes were held in a church basement and students lived in rented rooms in a private home. Today, partly because the college's very conception symbolized the end of a statewide Congregationalist monopoly in higher education, Trinity's charter prohibits religious standards from being imposed upon any student, faculty member or other member of the college community.

A year after opening, Trinity moved to its first campus, which consisted of two Greek Revival-style buildings, one housing a chapel, library and lecture rooms and the other a dormitory. Within a few years, the student body grew to nearly 100, a size that was rarely exceeded until the 20th century. In 1872, an important step toward the future was taken when the trustees sold the "College Hill" campus to the city of Hartford as the site for a new State Capitol. Six years later, the college moved to its present location.

The new site, known in the 18th century as Gallows Hill, was bordered on the west by a tree-lined bluff and by gently rolling fields to the east. The buildings that surround the main quadrangle, including the stunning Long Walk, were designed by noted English architect William Burges and are generally viewed as America's earliest examples of "collegiate Gothic" architecture. Together with the imposing Gothic chapel completed in 1932, they are a compelling reminder of the medieval origins of collegiate institutions.

Changing with the Times

In 1969, the trustees voted to admit women as undergraduates for the first time in the college's history. In September 1984, Trinity passed a milestone when it enrolled the first freshman class in its history in which

women outnumbered men. Coincident with these developments, the college has acted to increase the number of minority students on campus, as well as women and minority group members on the faculty and in the administration.

In 1995 the college began to focus its attention on the needs of the surrounding neighborhoods, spearheading a multifaceted revitalization initiative in partnership with community organizations. Central to that initiative is The Learning Corridor, which includes a public, Montessori-style elementary school, a neighborhood middle school, a math, science and art high school resource center to serve suburban as well as Hartford students and teachers, a center for families and child care, the first Boys & Girls Club in the country to be located at a college, and a health and technology center. Trinity students have numerous opportunities to engage in volunteer work, internships and research projects in conjunction with these institutions and other elements of the neighborhood initiative, as do members of the faculty.

A Quality Liberal Arts Education

Amid continuing change, Trinity's commitment to liberal education remains steadfast. The college is consistently ranked among the top liberal arts colleges in the nation. As a residential college situated on a historic 100-acre campus in Connecticut's capital, Trinity offers extensive opportunities for combining classroom instruction with experiential learning in the city. Its rigorous curriculum includes the traditional liberal arts disciplines as well as outstanding science, engineering and interdisciplinary programs.

The heart of Trinity's educational excellence is the personal encounter between professor and student. With a 10:1 faculty student ratio, this intellectual partnership opens a world of ideas and launches a lifelong pursuit of knowledge. With 37 majors and 970 courses to choose from, as well as an array of special curricular options, students explore many different paths to self-discovery. They are challenged to think critically and creatively and learn to develop effective communication and argumentation skills.

Making New Connections

Beyond its traditional strengths in the arts and the humanities, Trinity engages students in ongoing conversations through innovative academic programs like human rights, InterArts, interdisciplinary science, and the Tutorial College – "a college within a college" – where students and faculty from multiple disciplines explore the world

from varying perspectives. Two-thirds of the students take advantage of Trinity's urban connections and extensive internship opportunities – in government and non-profit organizations, global businesses and media companies. More than half study abroad on Trinity's campus in Rome, at one of the College's seven global learning sites, including Barcelona, Moscow and Cape Town, South Africa, or through other exchange programs around the world.

Trinity's 2,000 students come from all around the country and the world and become part of the diverse campus community. Trinity employs more than 600 faculty and staff, and the college is led by President James F. Jones, Jr. All members of the Trinity community benefit from a wealth of extracurricular offerings, including critically acclaimed films, plays and concerts, as well as lectures by internationally known speakers. They participate in cultural and community outreach activities and learn to celebrate differences. Most importantly, Trinity is the place where students can discover who they are and who they want to become.

For more information about Trinity, visit the college's Web site at *www.trincoll.edu*.

A GROUP OF STUDENTS IN AN ART CLASS WITH ASSOCIATE PROFESSOR OF FINE ARTS PABLO DELANO.

ASSOCIATE PROFESSOR OF PHYSICS BARBARA WALDEN AND STUDENTS CONDUCT AN EXPERIMENT ON ELECTRICITY AND MAGNETISM.

THE STANLEY WORKS

"The secret of this company's success is an open one – all who will may avail themselves of it, and all who do so will succeed – one word tells it all and that one word is – Excellence."

– Asher & Adam's Pictorial Album of American Industry, 1877

MAIN STREET, NEW BRITAIN, IN THE 1890S. THE STANLEY WORKS BEGAN HERE AND IS HEADQUARTERED IN THE SAME AREA TODAY.

*I*n New Britain, in a small, one-story wooden building, in 1843, Frederick T. Stanley partnered with his brother, William, to found The Stanley Bolt Manufactory. Business flourished, and immediately the Stanley brothers began to grow their business. Additions were added to the building to house the innovative new steam engine they had brought to Connecticut. More buildings housed additional equipment and increased manufacturing capacity. Demand steadily increased as Stanley's reputation for quality and value became widespread.

In 1852, Frederick and William Stanley took the next step, purchasing the building across the street from the Bolt Manufactory and forming a joint stock corporation with several other investors. This was the birth of The Stanley Works, a new and separate hardware manufacturing company that made high-quality hinges, bolts, hooks, staples and other hardware by casting and forging iron in a giant New Britain furnace.

Under the direction of William Hart, whom investors chose as treasurer and secretary and who soon became general manager, and Frederick Stanley, The Stanley Works continued to grow, tripling sales year over year and purchasing the original Bolt Manufactory to consolidate operations.

Throughout the Civil War, The Stanley Works doubled output to provide hinges, bolts, handles and other hardware for the Union Army. To keep up with competition following the war, Stanley built a three-story brick building on the site of the original wooden home to the Bolt Manufactory, and again increased manufacturing and breadth of product.

By 1870, Stanley owned several buildings throughout New Britain, a cast-iron butt manufacturing company based in Philadelphia, and enough land in New Britain to build more. Competitors began to fold, as Stanley's constant introduction of inventive new products, its unparalleled manufacturing capacity, and its unrivaled quality and value proved too much for com-petitors to take. Stanley was the No. 1 hardware manufacturer in the country.

Expansion continued. Stanley bought a copper rolling mill in Boston, opened a sales office in New York City, purchased a machinery manufacturer called Crooke & Company, bought out a Massachusetts-based tack manufacturer to begin making tacks and began construction on a New Britain manufacturing campus.

Another Stanley Tool Company

In 1857, as The Stanley Works was enjoying this growth, a company owned by Frederick Stanley's distant cousin, Henry, was also gaining a world-renowned reputation for quality. The Stanley Rule & Level Company, also based in New Britain, manufactured innovative and practical tools, including plumbs, levels, squares and rules. Stanley's reputation for accuracy made its marking tools the choice of professional builders, and the company grew quickly.

Soon, The Stanley Rule & Level Company had purchased another company, also owned by cousins of the Stanley family, which manufactured tool handles from ivory, hickory, rosewood and imported hardwoods.

The Stanley Rule & Level Company delivered new product after new product, and changed the way people work with tools. After purchasing a Boston-based company, Stanley introduced the Bailey plane, and quickly became not only the country's largest supplier of rules and levels, but also the world's largest maker of planes and related tools.

Then, Stanley purchased three small tool companies – the John S. Fray Company, of Bridgeport, Hurley & Wood Company, of

Plantsville, and Union Manufacturing Company, of New Britain. These three companies, coupled with Stanley's dominance in measuring and planing, gave Stanley a stronghold in the carpenters tools market. Stanley innovation and processes took root in these businesses, and Stanley began to deliver even more innovative, practical and high-quality tools.

The Stanley Rule & Level Company continued to grow, purchasing 15 companies, businesses and plants before World War I. Stanley became synonymous with quality tools, year after year delivering new products that strengthened its position as the leader in tools.

The Toolbox of America

As the two Stanley companies grew side by side in New Britain, both in complementary businesses, there seemed only one logical course of action. On May 1, 1920, The Stanley Works and The Stanley Rule & Level Company announced a merger that would make the new company, which kept the name The Stanley Works, the single strongest company in virtually every aspect of hand tools and hardware.

The new company immediately continued its predecessors' legacy of growth. The Stanley Works expanded into Europe with new plants in Germany and England that increased the scope of Stanley's reach. Even during the Great Depression, Stanley continued to acquire companies, most notably four electric tool manufacturers that complemented Stanley's own electric tool development, and together comprised The Stanley Electric Tool Company.

Innovations That Built A Company

In 1930 and 1931, Stanley's engineers, already recognized for their consistent innovation, developed two products that would take the company in new directions.

A small little "eye" peering down at pedestrians from atop a doorway automatically opened the door as they approached. And a small coiled steel tape with cross curvature allowed builders to fit six to eight feet of measuring tape into the palms of their hands.

Installed at the Wilcox Pier Restaurant in Savin Rock, the Stanley Magic Door was the first automatic door in the world, inviting guests in by swinging open, as if by "magic." Magic Doors were soon installed in Pennsylvania Station in New York City, and they took off from there.

While tape measures had been used before, they were floppy and ineffective.

Most professionals still used folding wooden rulers manufactured by Stanley's Eagle Square Company. With cross curvature, Stanley's tape measure stood out straight and included a spring to pull the blade back in. This patent, and Stanley's reputation for unparalleled accuracy, made Stanley the leader in tape measures that it remains today.

Growing With A Nation

Like most manufacturing companies during World War II, Stanley stepped up production and manufactured war munitions, using its New Britain facilities to create steel cups for ammunition cartridges, magazines, gas mask parts, and much more. By the time the war ended, Stanley was a manufacturing powerhouse, even more so than it had been before.

In the years immediately following the war, profits more than tripled. Stanley tools and hardware were building America's homes and buildings, supporting the boom in construction as soldiers came home.

Stanley led the do-it-yourself trend of the 1950s not only with the products that homeowners wanted, but also with tips and ads encouraging handymen to make improvements to their own homes. During this time, Stanley delivered new lines of products specifically geared toward do-it-yourselfers and made an indelible impression on the men and women of the time as the benchmark of quality tools.

And Stanley was continuing to grow. New plants in New Britain and new acquisitions strengthened the company's portfolio and reach. Stanley was now producing auger bits, garden tools, spiral and ratchet screwdrivers, and more, and had built five new buildings in New Britain, including a steel mill that increased the company's production by 50 percent.

Continued on next page

EMPLOYEES OF THE STANLEY RULE & LEVEL COMPANY GATHER OUTSIDE THE STANLEY OFFICES IN 1896.

COMBINING THE STANLEY WORKS AND THE STANLEY RULE & LEVEL COMPANY MADE STANLEY THE SINGLE STRONGEST COMPANY IN VIRTUALLY EVERY ASPECT OF HAND TOOLS AND HARDWARE.

THE STANLEY WORKS

Continued from previous page

STANLEY QUALITY SPEAKS FOR ITSELF. FROM A 1930S ADVERTISEMENT, TWO MEN ARE SUPPORTED ONLY BY A STANLEY HAMMER.

"EVEN A WORKING MODEL OF THE MAGIC DOOR IS INCLUDED IN THIS DISPLAY...HUNDREDS ARE VISITING IT DAILY AND MANY ARE ASTONISHED AT THE LITTLE LESS THAN ONE THOUSAND ITEMS DISPLAYED, ALL MANUFACTURED BY STANLEY." (THE STANLEY NEWS)

Going Global

Stanley capitalized on its strength in America to enhance its presence in the world. Beyond expanding the plants in Germany and England, Stanley formed joint ventures that extended its footprint into Australia, the Philippines, France, Holland, Italy, New Zealand and beyond.

Stanley also diversified. With dominance in the tools and hardware markets, Stanley took a chance on air tools, developing drills, screwdrivers, nutsetters and impact wrenches. The company was, by this time, manufacturing garage doors as well. And the new acquisition that would become Stanley-Vidmar propelled Stanley into the industrial storage market.

At the same time, Stanley officially listed on the New York Stock Exchange. The company had been publicly selling stock for more than a hundred years, and the move to listing was popular with investors. Since then, Stanley has earned the distinction of having the longest continual period of both annual and quarterly dividends of any industrial company listed on the exchange.

Stanley continued its global focus. In the decades to follow, Stanley would increase its presence all over the world, with current operations in 134 countries on nearly every continent.

A Portfolio of Companies

The Stanley brand remained strong, a symbol of quality, innovative tools and hardware for consumers and professionals alike.

While earlier acquisitions bolstered Stanley's tools and hardware businesses, Stanley began to focus on expanding the breadth of its offerings.

After adding the Stanley-Vidmar industrial storage business, Stanley purchased MAC Tools, a top-quality mechanics tools company. Stanley was now in the automotive mechanics market, rather than focusing on carpenters tools.

Stanley added Proto, a big name in industrial sockets and wrenches. Stanley-Proto manufactures industrial grade tools and storage solutions for heavy-duty production and maintenance applications. Its products are used globally in auto, steel and airplane manufacturing, chemical plants, refineries, and transportation.

Bostitch was the next acquisition. Stanley-Bostitch makes fastening tools, like staplers and staple-guns, and specializes in air-powered nail guns and bindery stitchers. The Stanley Works had added another business that perfectly complemented its core tools market.

In relatively short order, Stanley acquired the Goldblatt Tool Company, makers of top-quality masonry tools, Jensen Tools, a precision tool maker, and LaBounty Manufacturing Inc., a manufacturer of large hydraulic tools.

Stanley Today

A sophisticated global corporation, Stanley has come a long way from the original wooden building bought by Frederick T. Stanley and his brother in 1843. But Stanley's dedication to quality, value and innovation has always remained the same. Currently, Stanley is a nearly $3 billion global corporation that employs more than 15,000 people in countries all across the world. Stanley consistently earns awards like Vendor of the Year and Innovator of the Year from the Golden Hammer Awards Committee, and IDEA (Industrial Design Excellence Award) from *BusinessWeek* magazine and the Industrial Designers Society of America. The frequency and caliber of these awards attest to Stanley's superior customer service and relentless innovation.

One Stanley – Seven Businesses

Stanley Tools Group: The tools that built the company are still a major focus at Stanley. In carpenters tools, mechanics tools, hardware, home décor products and more, Stanley means quality to the millions of consumers and professionals who use its tools every day. Stanley continues its legacy of innovation by consistently developing new practical, durable, high-quality tools for professional, consumer and industrial markets.

Stanley Security Solutions: Stanley's sec-

ond core focus is its Security Solutions Group, moving the company into the future with technology-focused systems and solutions. Stanley's Security Solutions Group develops, installs and supports the products that protect buildings, airports and institutions around the world, including automatic doors, integrated security and lock systems, touch screen security control systems, advanced event detectors, and much more.

Stanley Assembly Technologies: After taking a chance on the air tools business in the early 1960s, Stanley grew the Assembly Technologies business rapidly. Now, Stanley tools are used to build nearly every car, truck and SUV manufactured in the United States.

Stanley Fastening Systems: The choice of industrial and construction professionals everywhere, Stanley Bostitch fastening systems deliver a multitude of fastening products. From office staples and staplers to heavy duty pneumatic framing and roofing guns, Stanley Bostitch delivers durable, dependable products in all areas of fastening.

Stanley Hydraulic Tools: Under the names Stanley, LaBounty and Lynx, Stanley manufactures industrial strength hydraulic breakers, pumps, drills, saws and more. Stanley Hydraulics are powerful, rugged tools for construction and demolition experts.

Stanley Specialty Tools: A combination of Contact East and Jensen Tools, Stanley Specialty Tools supplies tool kits for assembling, repairing and testing electronic equipment, as well as products and equipment needed by technicians and service personnel in electronics and communications industries.

Mac Tools: Mac Tools is the leader in the professional hand tools industry, building lifelong relationships with its valued customers through a direct distribution model that has remained unchanged throughout its nearly 70-year history. Mac's philosophy of excellent quality, price and service also remains unchanged over the years, and the company spirit that made it successful in 1938 is the same spirit that makes the company a leader in the automotive tool and equipment business today.

Make Something Great™

Across all business units, The Stanley Works is still committed to the principles that helped it become the global leader in tools: Stanley delivers the highest quality products, the most comprehensive services and the best possible value. Stanley continues to lead the industry in product innovation, producing hundreds of practical, original new products every year.

Stanley further continues to play a large part in the communities that have supported its growth over the years. On both a local and national level, Stanley is deeply involved in charitable and community work, supporting large organizations like Habitat for Humanity – building homes for underprivileged homeowners – and SkillsUSA – supporting the development and growth of high school and college students striving for a career in the trades – and supporting small organizations, like the New Britain Rotary – with whom it has been involved for more than a hundred years – and the United Way chapters in each of its United States locations.

The Stanley Works is firmly committed to the future. With its proud past to build on, Stanley continually looks for growth opportunities. In the past year, Stanley acquired three new companies, strengthening the Stanley Tools Group and the Stanley Security Solutions Group. Always a part of the Stanley growth strategy, acquisitions now supplement organic growth to give The Stanley Works an even brighter outlook for the future. With strong earnings, strong products and strong strategies, The Stanley Works stands poised for a future of continued growth.

NOW, STANLEY® FATMAX™ TOOLS ARE THE CHOICE FOR PROFESSIONALS WHO RELY ON THE QUALITY, DURABILITY AND ACCURACY THAT HELPED STANLEY BUILD ITS NAME.

THE FUTURE IS HERE. STANLEY SECURITY SOLUTIONS PROTECTS BUILDINGS, AIRPORTS AND INSTITUTIONS AROUND THE WORLD WITH STATE-OF-THE-ART ACCESS AND SECURITY TECHNOLOGY.

MCCARTER & ENGLISH LLP

The Hartford office of

McCarter & English

represents the combination

of attorneys from two highly

respected legal firms with

more than two centuries

of service to clients

throughout Connecticut

and the country.

PHOTO/STEVE LASCHEVER

ATTORNEYS (FROM LEFT)
MOY OGILVIE, JASON WELCH,
ERIC WATT WIECHMANN,
CATHERINE MOHAN, JANE
WARREN AND JOHN ROBINSON
ON THE STEPS OF CITYPLACE
WHERE MCCARTER & ENGLISH'S
OFFICES ARE LOCATED IN
CITYPLACE I ON THE 36TH
AND 37TH FLOORS.

McCarter & English LLP in Hartford is actually the story of two great legal firms brought together by their longstanding histories and an unparalleled tradition of client service. From its earliest beginnings, McCarter & English and Cummings & Lockwood seemed destined to join together. Thomas Nesbitt McCarter began practicing law in 1843 in Newark, New Jersey, and in 1906 his son, Robert, was joined by Conover English. At approximately the same time, two Connecticut friends, Homer Cummings and Charles Lockwood, opened their law practice in Stamford three years later in 1909.

The accomplishments of both firms grew, as did their reputations. As the oldest and largest law firm in New Jersey, McCarter & English's legacy spans more than 160 years (Conover English represented such famous clients as Thomas A. Edison); while as one of the oldest firms in Connecticut, Cummings & Lockwood LLC has offered clients a century of success.

Lawyers from both firms have also played leading roles in the evolution of business throughout the Northeast and the U.S. McCarter & English partners played integral roles in the World War II U. S. Savings Bond Campaign and New Jersey Turnpike Authority. Cummings & Lockwood's Homer Cummings was Chairman of the Democratic Party from 1913-1921 and served as Attorney General in the cabinet of President Franklin Roosevelt. In that role, he established the Federal Rules of Civil Procedure.

The merger of McCarter & English with Cummings & Lockwood's Hartford office in 2003 reflected mutual industry commit-

ments, as well as shared depth in intellectual property, business litigation, transactional work, and national toxic tort and product liability. Drawing on McCarter & English's resources, track record and offices throughout the Northeast Corridor – including New York, Philadelphia, Newark, Stamford, Wilmington and Baltimore – the Hartford office has been able to accomplish an even wider array of goals on behalf of its clients. The firm's combined 300+ attorneys are known for their skill and strategic insights with challenges that exist in six core industry areas: Financial Services, Life Sciences, Technology, Consumer & Industrial Products, Mid-Cap Companies and Private Client matters. Today, McCarter & English's Hartford office has grown to become a nationally recognized leader among Fortune 500 companies, mid-cap firms and private businesses located throughout Connecticut and the country.

While the firm continues its tradition of service to clients throughout the Northeast, McCarter & English also has a commitment to civic and charitable organizations in its surrounding communities. The Hartford office supports the MetroHartford Alliance, the Connecticut Business and Industry Association, the Connecticut Technology Council, as well as numerous industry professional associations, particularly in the construction arena. In addition, McCarter & English is a proud corporate sponsor of the Greater Hartford Arts Council, the Bushnell Center for the Performing Arts and The Greater Hartford Legal Aid Foundation.

McCarter & English's Hartford office is located on the 36th and 37th floors of CityPlace I. Visit the firm's website at *www.mccarter.com.*

COLT GATEWAY

For more than 150 years, the blue onion dome of the Colt historic landmark has adorned Hartford's southern skyline.

(ABOVE) A VIEW OF DOWNTOWN HARTFORD FROM THE COLT COMPLEX.

(BELOW) AN AERIAL VIEW RENDERING OF COLT GATEWAY OVERLOOKING THE CONNECTICUT RIVER.

Since its completion in 1847, the dome has been a symbol of Hartford's ingenuity and the industrial and technological innovations that changed the way of life in America.

The Colt Gateway site, listed on the National Register of Historic Places, is currently applying for National Park designation. The history of Coltsville is one of industrial innovation and technological development. It was here in the 1800s that Samuel and Elizabeth Colt created the firearms factory that was a catalyst for a technological revolution with Hartford at its center.

"People look at Colt as being representative of all the great industrial work that occurred in Connecticut. You had bicycles made here. You had typewriters made here. It was a special period of time for Hartford. It's our vision to bring this ingenuity back to Hartford through Colt Gateway," says Robert MacFarlane, president and CEO of Homes for America Holdings Inc.

Colt Gateway, a subsidiary of Homes for America Holdings Inc., a real estate company that specializes in the revitalization of neighborhoods and cities, has begun the $110 million historic restoration of Coltsville. The master plan is to transform the 17-acre site into a thriving community with commercial, residential and retail space. The community features 10 distinct buildings with century-old architectural accents like exposed brick, wooden beams, spiral staircases and cathedral ceilings, integrated with modern facilities and amenities. The community will house a visitors' center, museum and a park-like setting with greenscapes and gardens with a seasonal pond/ice-rink.

Expected to be completed in 2006, the Colt Gateway Community will be connected to Hartford's downtown entertainment district, Adriaen's Landing and the Connecticut River offering a variety of activities and attractions.

PHOTO ILLUSTRATION/TAI SOO KIM PARTNERS

THE MARK TWAIN HOUSE & MUSEUM

Mark Twain – author, humorist, lecturer and social critic – was an incorrigible self-promoter. He wrote in 1909, "One of my high ideals ... is to remain indestructible in a perishable world."

PHOTO/JEFFREY YARDIS

"OF ALL THE BEAUTIFUL TOWNS THAT IT HAS BEEN MY FORTUNE TO SEE, THIS IS THE CHIEF," MARK TWAIN SAID THE FIRST TIME HE SAW HARTFORD. FOR 17 YEARS, TWAIN AND HIS FAMILY LIVED IN THIS UNIQUE HOUSE IN THE CITY'S WEST END WHERE HE WROTE "ADVENTURES OF HUCKLEBERRY FINN" AND OTHER GREAT WORKS.

Twain's wit and wisdom has endured, and a new museum in the backyard of his beloved Hartford home is enhancing the legacy of one of America's most revered icons – and helping Twain remain indestructible.

Mark Twain, born Samuel Langhorne Clemens, first visited Hartford in 1868, shortly after the publication of "The Celebrated Jumping Frog of Calaveras County." He was a restless, 32-year-old former riverboat pilot and gold prospector who had finally found steady income as a newspaper correspondent and lecturer. In Hartford to visit the publisher of his first travelogue, "The Innocents Abroad," Twain was also in the midst of another momentous occasion in his life, the courtship of Olivia Langdon of Elmira, N.Y.

Sam and Livy were married in 1870 and moved to Hartford in 1871 to be near his publisher, the American Publishing Co. The family first rented a house on Forest Street in Nook Farm from Livy's friends, John and Isabella Beecher Hooker, and later purchased land on Farmington Avenue, where their neighbors were some of Hartford's most prominent citizens. In 1873, they

engaged New York City architect Edward Tuckerman Potter to design the house. Livy sketched a layout which related the various rooms to views over what was then open countryside and a bend, or nook, in the Park River. The cost apparently exceeded their budget and the interior of the home remained unfinished when the family moved in October 1874. The house was a treasure for the Clemens family. Twain wrote:

"To us, our house . . . had a heart, and a soul, and eyes to see us with; and approvals and solicitudes and deep sympathies; it was of us, and we were in its confidence and lived in its grace and in the peace of it benediction."

In 1881, the success of "The Adventures of Tom Sawyer" and several lecture tours allowed Twain and his wife to enlarge the home's servants' wing and hire Louis Comfort Tiffany's design firm, Associated Artists, to decorate the home's first floor.

Even as his fame grew from his writings and his lecture tours across the United States and Europe, Twain always returned to his home on Farmington Avenue in Hartford where he and Livy raised their three daughters, Susy, Clara and Jean.

Twain often referred to his years in Hartford as the happiest and most productive of his life. During his 17 years at his Farmington Avenue home, he wrote several major works – including "Life on The Mississippi" (1883), "Adventures of Huckleberry Finn" (1884), and "A Connecticut Yankee in King Arthur's Court" (1889) – that would redefine modern American literature.

Financial problems forced Sam and Livy to move the family to Europe in 1891. Though he would complain about the other places the family lived ("How ugly, tasteless, repulsive are all the domestic interiors I have ever seen in Europe compared with the perfect taste of this [the Hartford home's] ground floor"), the family never lived in Hartford again. Susy's death in 1896 made it too hard for Livy to return to their Hartford home and they sold the property in 1903.

Twain's remarkable 19-room Victorian mansion changed owners several times after the turn of the century. It was used as a private school and an apartment building. In 1919, a group of local citizens recognized the house's historic importance and developed plans to preserve the home. Ten years later, the Mark Twain Memorial and Library Commission saved the house from a developer's wrecking ball and purchased the property. The house served as the Mark Twain branch of the Hartford Public Library for many years before a total restoration began in the 1950s. In the 1960s, the Mark Twain House was opened as a museum under the auspices of the Mark Twain Memorial, the private, nonprofit organization that still owns and operates the museum.

The Mark Twain House was designated a National Historic Landmark in 1963 and is the winner of a major award for restoration from the National Trust for Historic Preservation. The house contains many pieces of Clemens' family furniture, including Twain's ornate Venetian bed, an intricately carved mantel from a Scottish castle, and a billiard table owned by the author.

Now open year-round for guided tours, The Mark Twain House & Museum attracts more than 65,000 visitors a year and is one of the premier tourist attractions in Connecticut. Because of the international notoriety of Twain, The Mark Twain House & Museum attracts visitors from every state in the nation as well as from more than 70 countries around the world. In addition to opening the historic house for tours, the organization also runs

PHOTO/HUNTER NEAL

dozens of special programs about Twain's writing, his family life and the literary elite who lived in Connecticut during Twain's time, including his Nook Farm neighbor, Harriet Beecher Stowe.

As it passes the century mark since Twain's ownership, the Mark Twain House & Museum has completed the most ambitious project since the initial restoration of the house. In November 2003, the institution opened its Museum Center, a 33,000-square-foot building that offers a more enhanced visitor experience and a deeper appreciation of Twain's life, times and achievements.

An exhibition about Twain's life and times, "I Have Sampled This Life," displays treasured Twain artifacts, including souvenirs from his world travels, the bicycle that he tried to ride (hilariously recounted in his essay, "Taming the Bicycle"), and the four-ton mechanical typesetter, an investment which drove Twain into bankruptcy and forced him from his Hartford home. The building also has a gallery for changing exhibits and new attractions for tourists.

Of course, there's plenty of Twain throughout the new building in the form of his observations on life, including: "When in doubt, tell the truth," "The lack of money is the root of all evil," "Always respect your superiors, if you have any," and "Always do right. This will gratify some people and astonish the rest." These words are carved in the limestone walls of the building's interior. There may be no better way to remain "indestructible in a perishable world."

MARK TWAIN'S WORDS ARE ETCHED IN THE WALLS OF THE NEW MUSEUM CENTER AT THE MARK TWAIN HOUSE & MUSEUM. THE CENTER FEATURES A FILM BY KEN BURNS THAT PREPARES VISITORS FOR A TOUR OF TWAIN'S VICTORIAN HOME.

PARKER FLUID CONTROL DIVISION

With its earliest predecessor dating back to 1885, the Parker Fluid Control Division (FCD) of Parker Hannifin Corporation has undergone a series of changes in name and ownership, but its mission and successes have remained strong.

THE FRONT ENTRANCE OF PARKER FLUID CONTROL DIVISION. FCD IS LOCATED AT 95 EDGEWOOD AVENUE IN NEW BRITAIN, CONNECTICUT.

*P*arker Fluid Control Division's quality policy is "to meet or exceed our customers' expectations through continuous improvement and the elimination of waste." This policy statement has remained consistently strong throughout its history and has brought repeated success. Headquartered in New Britain, Parker Fluid Control Division produces multiple lines of high-quality solenoid valves that provide innovative solutions for clients in the climate and industrial control markets. The company, which also has a manufacturing facility in Madison, Miss., and "sister" operations in Geneva, Switzerland, and Milan, Italy, markets its valves to the industrial sector.

Solenoid valves are integral parts of a variety of common, everyday products. A solenoid valve is an electromechanical device that controls the flow of a refrigerant, water or light oil. Washing machines, dishwashers, icemakers and other household devices that are owned by the average consumer all use solenoid valves. People also come across them when they pump gas, use copy machines or brew a cup of coffee.

FCD manufactures solenoid and process control valves for eight different market segments: commercial equipment, fuel dispensing, medical and instrumentation, automotive, industrial equipment, process control, HVAC and refrigeration. There are numerous applications that need these valves, such as cooking and food warming equipment, beverage dispensing, blood pressure devices, sterilizers, nitrous oxide, fire protection systems and food processing. These are just a few of the applications that require solenoid and process control valves. Everyday, people come into contact with solenoid or process control valves. For example, when going out to dinner, the dishes have been cleaned by utilizing a solenoid valve to control the water that cleans the plate. When ordering a hot cup of coffee, valves are used to control the steam and hot water to brew the coffee to perfection. Solenoid and process control valves are utilized every single day from your morning cup of coffee or latte from your favorite coffee shop to the gas station down the street that shuts off your gas at the exact amount you prepaid.

Parker Fluid Control Division has been a part of the New Britain area stemming back as early as 1887. Although the company has undergone numerous name changes throughout the years, its vision remains steadfast. FCD's vision is "to be recognized as the Premier Provider of Innovative Fluid Control Products, Value Added Assemblies and System Solutions to the OEM and Industrial Markets."

Parker FCD is the manufacturer of Skinner Valve™, Jackes Evans™, Gold Ring™ and Sinclair Collins™ products, with plants here, in New Britain, as well as Madison, Miss.

For almost 120 years FCD, formerly known as Skinner Chuck Company, Skinner Electric and Skinner Valve, has made New Britain its home, whether machining chucks, in 1887, or manufacturing solenoid valves today. With six distinct product lines, the company's name now reflects that there is a valve available for practically any application. As Parker's Fluid Control Division, the company's vast capabilities are clear, from solenoid to process control valves.

These years of experience have made Parker Fluid Control Division a global leader in the production of these valves. From its early days as Skinner Valve, the company nurtured a reputation for making the highest quality solenoid valves on the market. By combining six distinct product lines and growing into the Fluid Control Division, the firm built upon the existing capabilities of each. Innovation continues with multiple new products launched, further extending the company's product lines and expanding its customer base.

Today, the company is headquartered in New Britain, where 204 employees work in a 150,000-square-foot facility of manufacturing, assembly, sales and administrative space. The New Britain site specializes in laser welding, machining, assembly and the testing of valves. Most recently, the operation formed a Fuel Cell Systems Business Unit to develop products and systems for the emerging fuel cell markets.

The Madison, Miss., branch boasts a 60,000-square-foot facility comprised of manufacturing, assembly and administrative space. More than 140 employees work there, specializing in machining, brazing, assembly and testing.

Together, the division's manufacturing sites produce valves that travel to more than 250 distributors across the country, as well as customers and distributors across the globe. As part of the larger Parker

Hannifin Corporation, the FCD's market comprises about 10 percent of the company's total revenue, which exceeds $7 billion annually.

Parker Hannifin Corporation is a diversified manufacturer of motion and control technologies that provides systematic, precision-engineered solutions for a wide variety of commercial, mobile, industrial and aerospace markets.

Parker Hannifin employs more than 48,000 people in 44 countries around the world. It serves numerous well-known clients that are among the leaders in global manufacturing including Ford, General Electric, John Deere, Chrysler, Wal-Mart, Xerox, Lennox, Carrier, York International Corp., Hill Phoenix, Tokheim, Rheem, Scotsman, Trane, Tyler Refrigeration Corp., Hussman, Goodman and Freightliner.

The Fluid Control Division's associates work diligently to meet or exceed customers' expectations. As a result, customers continually receive the top-quality products and service they have grown to expect from FCD, just as they have throughout its nearly 120-year history, as FCD strives to be a leading worldwide manufacturer of fluid control components and systems. With every name change that FCD has undergone, one thing remains the same: FCD is proud to call New Britain its home and looks forward to the next 120 years.

A PORTION OF THE SHIPPING AREA OF PARKER FLUID CONTROL DIVISION IS SHOWN HERE. PARKER EMPLOYEES, JANINA SHOREY AND TERESA URBANSKI ARE PREPARING ORDERS FOR SHIPMENT.

EDWARDS & ANGELL LLP

Founded in 1894 by Walter Angell and Stephen Edwards in Providence, R.I., Edwards & Angell LLP has grown to become a nationally recognized, full-service law firm.

PHOTO/STEVE LASCHEVER

EDWARDS & ANGELL LLP HAS BEEN A LONG-TIME SUPPORTER OF THE PERFORMING ARTS. PICTURED ABOVE AT THE BUSHNELL CENTER FOR THE PERFORMING ARTS ARE, FROM LEFT, FIRM MEMBERS MICHAEL T. GRIFFIN, JOHN H. REID III, CHARLES R. WELSH, AND JOHN N. EMMANUEL.

The firm's culture encourages a strong interdisciplinary approach to client service. This allows the firm to bring together attorneys from multiple practice areas, combining knowledge and improved responsiveness for each client's unique need. Located in nine major U.S. commercial centers, as well as a representative office in London, England, the firm employs more than 325 attorneys and 480 highly professional administrators, paralegals and support staff, and it's still growing. In 2003 and 2004, the firm opened offices in Stamford, Conn., and Wilmington, Del.

Until the mid-1980s, the firm's practice catered to New England-based businesses and investors. Over the past 20 years, as the firm expanded its geographic base, it developed a national and international practice in three specific areas: financial services, private equity and venture capital/technology. Indeed, it was because of the firm's commitment to the financial services industry that Edwards & Angell established the Hartford office in 1991. Beginning with two Providence attorneys and two Hartford attorneys, the Hartford office has grown to 25 attorneys. Seeking to increase its presence in the state and recognizing the diversity of Connecticut's business community, Edwards & Angell opened the Stamford office in 2003. The firm now has more than 50 attorneys in Connecticut and anticipates future measured growth. Its Connecticut lawyers have been involved in large financial transactions such as mergers in the insurance and banking industries, commercial real estate deals and complex commercial litigation cases. They also advise individual clients on a variety of tax, business and financial issues, as well as represent them in state and federal litigation.

Attorneys continually remain ahead of the curve and provide their clients with fresh and unique perspectives on the world's ever-changing economic, regulatory, social and political issues. By doing so, the firm's clients are empowered to anticipate, adapt and quickly respond to the challenges that they face today.

The establishment of an insurance practice division is one of the many highlights of the firm's Hartford office. In 1992, the firm did not even have an insurance practice; today its insurance and reinsurance department is one of its fastest growing practice areas. Its client list numbers in the hundreds of companies, many of them well-known names, both in Connecticut and abroad. Its publications are well recognized. Its insurance lawyers and analysts are active in the National Association of Insurance Commissioners and other industry groups. The firm's attorneys enjoy national and international reputations in the insurance field, and have been specifically recognized in the industry's major publications. Edwards & Angell has well-established relationships with significant firms in London and Bermuda, and with highly regarded lawyers and consultants in the important insurance and commercial centers throughout the world. Because of the firm's internationally recognized experience, it has assisted in legal proceedings and transactions in England, Canada, Bermuda, Switzerland, France, Ireland, Italy and other countries. The founding of its insurance practice in a city, which, for many years, billed itself as the "insurance capital of the U.S.," seems quite appropriate.

Edwards & Angell provides hands-on, partner level involvement with a team of associates and legal assistants appropriate for the transaction size, complexity and timetable. It helps structure transactions and negotiate and document transactions in accordance with clients' goals. Its attorneys believe it is their job to facilitate the closing of transactions. Although their work product is legal services, they never lose sight of their clients' objectives. Their state-of-the-art communications, case management and document storage technologies enable them to handle the most complex matters successfully and economically. However, it is ultimately the quality of the lawyers' combined decades of experience that distinguishes Edwards & Angell and assures its clients the highly skilled representation they require.

Edwards & Angell has earned a reputation as a distinguished community leader. The firm encourages participation in community-based charitable, educational and civic organizations. Its attorneys serve as chairmen, overseers, directors and advisors to numerous Hartford area community organizations and nonprofit corporations. Its lawyers teach at the University of Connecticut Law School and are active in state bar association activities. From the beginning, the Hartford office has been a supporter of the performing and intellectual arts through long-term sponsorships of The

Bushnell Center for the Performing Arts, one of the nation's leading cultural centers, through the Edwards & Angell Off-Broadway Series. From the Connecticut Forum, which provides an opportunity for civic leaders, writers, government leaders and entertainers to address broad issues that affect our community and nation, to the Greater Hartford Arts Council and Wadsworth Atheneum, Edwards & Angell believes that Hartford offers superb educational and cultural opportunities and sees those opportunities as the building blocks of the city's future. It also contributes to organizations that directly support individuals and families in need in the Hartford area, such as the South Park Inn, United Way, American Cancer Society and other deserving charities.

Guide. Advise. Protect.

These are the leading principles for more than 325 attorneys who make up Edwards & Angell LLP. Fortune 1,000 corporations, financial institutions, emerging companies and individuals alike look to Edwards & Angell's lawyers to guide them through their legal obstacles, advise them on the best course of action and protect them from hazards. Not only are these the standards that the firm adopted long ago to ensure the trust and confidence of its clients, these are also the standards that make Edwards & Angell a leader in each community that it serves.

For more information about Edwards & Angell, visit the firm's website at *www.EdwardsAngell.com.*

EDWARDS & ANGELL LLP SUPPORTS MANY LOCAL CHARITABLE ORGANIZATIONS. PICTURED ABOVE AT THE SOUTH PARK INN ARE THEODORE P. AUGUSTINOS AND JANET M. HELMKE.

SAINT FRANCIS HOSPITAL AND MEDICAL CENTER

Since its founding in 1897 by the Sisters of Saint Joseph of Chambéry, Saint Francis Hospital and Medical Center has developed a national reputation for medical excellence, technological innovation and a caring compassion for its patients.

A HOSPITAL WITHIN A HOSPITAL, THE PATIENT CARE TOWER AT SAINT FRANCIS TODAY IS ONE OF THE MOST CONTEMPORARY MEDICAL FACILITIES IN THE REGION.

One of Connecticut's largest hospitals, Saint Francis is the largest Catholic hospital in New England. With clinical concentrations in cardiology, oncology, women's health services, rehabilitation and orthopedics, Saint Francis provides sophisticated, contemporary medicine to the Greater Hartford community. The hospital is a leader in the use of clinical information technology and has the most advanced imaging equipment available.

Saint Francis has been named among the top 100 hospitals and the top 15 major teaching hospitals in the United States six times by Solucient, a leading health care research firm. Saint Francis is the only major teaching hospital in the Northeast to be named a Top 100 hospital on six or more occasions.

When it opened in Hartford's Asylum Hill neighborhood, Saint Francis accommodated 30 patients in its wards. Its first administrator was a nun from France, Mother Valencia, who barely spoke English. Mother Valencia and the other sisters came with less than $10 between them. Strongly championing the new hospital, physicians themselves went door to door seeking donations. While most patients were charged a fee of $15 per week, others received discounted rates because of their low income, and many were given care on credit.

From its inception, the hospital has responded to the region's health care needs, notably in providing critical care during the 1903 outbreak of scarlet fever when health care workers endangered their own lives to attend to victims, and in 1919 when it was designated an Army Reserve hospital. When World War II began, Saint Francis was the first local hospital to initiate a Volunteer Red Cross Nurses Aid course.

Following World War II, the staff regrouped and began a new era that focused heavily on patient care and physician and nursing training. During the 1950s outbreak of polio, it was first in the area to establish a post-polio program. By the mid '50s, the hospital had established 11 separate specialized departments including pathology, radiology, outpatient services, cardiology and obstetrics.

Throughout the next three decades, Saint Francis continued to grow and enhance its services and programs. A laboratory for cardiopulmonary research, units for intensive care, coronary care and neonatal intensive care, centers for diabetes and ambulatory care, and a section for oncology were established. To reflect this expanding breadth of service, the hospital's name was changed to Saint Francis Hospital and Medical Center in 1976.

David D'Eramo, Ph.D., became the hospital's first lay president and CEO in 1988. Since then, Saint Francis has experienced tremendous growth in its clinical programs, propelling the hospital into the national spotlight in areas such as heart, cancer and women's services.

In 1990, Saint Francis formed an affiliation with Mount Sinai Hospital, believed to be the first such collaboration between a

Catholic hospital and a Jewish hospital in U.S. history, culminating in a formal corporate merger in 1995.

The establishment of the Hoffman Heart Institute in 1991 was a significant development in the evolution of the hospital's cardiology program. Named in recognition of the grant from the Maximilian E. and Marion O. Hoffman Foundation, the institute focuses on areas of prevention, diagnosis and treatment of cardiovascular diseases, as well as the rehabilitation of patients with the disease. Cardio-thoracic surgeons now perform approximately 1,400 open-heart surgeries annually, more than any other hospital in Connecticut. In 2002, Saint Francis was the only hospital in the state to be named one of the nation's Top 100 Hospitals for cardiovascular services.

In 1993, the Saint Francis/Mount Sinai Regional Cancer Center was opened. The facility, made possible through a significant contribution from the Mount Sinai Hospital Foundation, houses the latest technology such as a state-of-the-art linear accelerator and chemotherapeutic facilities. Today, disease-specific services for patients with various types of cancer are organized to provide a multi-disciplinary treatment approach.

Greatly advancing women's health services, the John M. Gibbons Pavilion opened in 1996. Located in the Pavilion are 14 labor-delivery-recovery rooms, an antepartum evaluation and diagnostic center, and a 28-bed neonatal intensive care unit. Approximately 3,400 deliveries are performed there each year. The Pavilion also contains a fully equipped ultrasound laboratory.

To further enhance women's health services at Saint Francis, the Comprehensive Breast Health Center was established in 1999. As part of Saint Francis' outpatient mission, this center eases the diagnosis process for women. On-site clinicians are able to provide a complete diagnosis and treatment plan in a single visit. The center became the first in Connecticut to offer computer-aided detection, which helps to identify hard-to-detect forms of breast cancer.

During the 1990s, Saint Francis continued to expand its continuum of care by affiliating with neighboring health care institutions. In 1995, Bristol Hospital and Saint Francis Hospital and Medical Center joined forces and in 1996, an affiliation agreement was signed with St. Mary's Hospital in Waterbury. Later affiliations included the

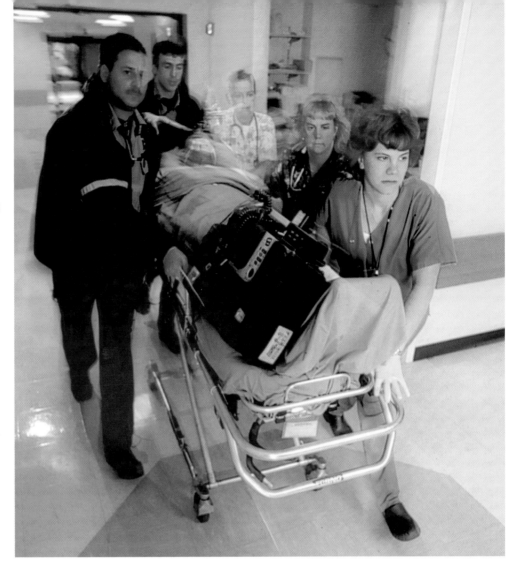

Greater Hartford Easter Seals Rehabilitation Center Inc., the Alcohol and Drug Recovery Center and the Suffield VNA.

More than just corporate or economic reorganizations, these affiliations created tangible improvements to the medical care of area residents. As an anchor institution in a multicultural, metropolitan area, Saint Francis has evolved to embrace the diversity of Connecticut's communities.

As Saint Francis entered the new millennium, it recognized that health consumers are taking a more active role in seeking medical information and making decisions that affect their health. Answering to these expectations, Saint Francis created a Department of Quality and Benchmarking in 2002.

Although Saint Francis places a great emphasis on utilizing the latest technology and equipment, it takes special care to remain steadfast in its mission and core values upon which it was founded more than a century ago. These include an unwavering commitment to compassion, charity, sensitivity and attentiveness – the values that underlie the basic desire to help those in need.

AT THE LEADING EDGE IN LIFESAVING CARE, AN EMERGENCY DEPARTMENT NURSE ASSISTS EMERGENCY MEDICAL TECHNICIANS IN TRANSPORTING A CRITICALLY ILL PATIENT FROM THE HOSPITAL'S HELIPAD.

The American Red Cross is in an enviable position – the Charter Oak Chapter and the Connecticut Blood Services Region are the local presence of one of the finest humanitarian organizations in the world.

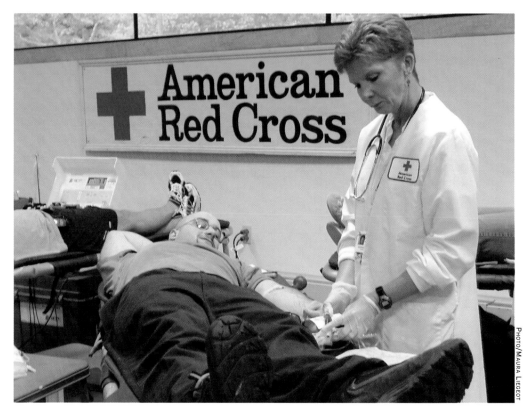

A NURSE COLLECTS BLOOD FROM A VOLUNTEER DONOR AT THE RED CROSS' BLOOD CENTER IN FARMINGTON. SINCE 1950, THE RED CROSS HAS BEEN PROVIDING BLOOD PRODUCTS TO CONNECTICUT HOSPITALS. TODAY, MORE THAN 600 PINTS OF BLOOD MUST BE COLLECTED DAILY TO MEET PATIENT NEEDS.

While it is fortunate that so many people recognize and respond to the trusted Red Cross symbol, this visibility represents an awesome responsibility.

The Red Cross was challenged with the mission of helping people prevent, prepare for and respond to emergencies in the Hartford area when it received its charter in 1906. Today, as it did in the early 1900s, the organization relies on the generosity of the public to enable it to fulfill its mission. The American public, not the government, supports the Red Cross through financial donations and volunteer services.

Through its vital biomedical services and chapter programs, the Red Cross helps countless individuals each day in Hartford communities and beyond. For every disaster client or accident victim helped by the organization and its volunteers, many others have averted tragedy because they have had Red Cross training.

Today, the Red Cross is focused on preparedness. Driven by its volunteers, the organization is working together with local hospitals and human service organizations to help prepare its communities for the unexpected. In doing so, the Red Cross strives to educate the public about the importance of Red Cross services available in Connecticut.

Emergency Services

When a fire threatens to leave people homeless, the Charter Oak Chapter of the American Red Cross is there. When an aviation accident occurs or an ice storm knocks out the power, the Red Cross is there. These are emergencies that occur day in and day out, no matter what other crises Connecticut residents are facing.

As soon as the alarm goes out to the fire department, Red Cross emergency services responders answer the call. Long after the fire is extinguished or the power lines are repaired, Red Cross volunteers continue to provide support and tangible help. Volunteers make sure those affected have temporary housing and meals to eat. They help replace vital medications and clothing. Red Cross representatives also counsel those who have suffered loss or have been affected emotionally by disaster. Most importantly, these dedicated people continue to work with displaced individuals and families until they are back on their feet.

Blood Services

Every day in Connecticut, hundreds of patients rely on donated blood for the treatments they need to improve – or save – their lives. The state's sole provider of this precious gift of life, the American Red Cross, Connecticut Blood Services Region, has the critical mission of providing a safe and adequate blood supply for patients at the state's 31 transfusing hospitals.

To accomplish this vital public service – and meet the constant demand for blood – the Red Cross relies entirely on the generosity of volunteer blood donors. Each day, Red Cross workers and volunteers span the state to hold blood drives that collect an average of 600 pints of whole blood per day. The blood is received at the Blood Center in Farmington, where each unit of whole blood is separated into three components: platelets, plasma and red cells. At the same time, test tubes from each pint are sent to a Red Cross laboratory in Dedham, Mass., for complete testing, which includes determining blood type and screening for infectious diseases such as HIV, hepatitis and syphilis.

Donated blood is used to treat accident and burn victims, premature babies and their mothers, surgery patients, people struggling with sickle cell disease, and cancer patients receiving chemotherapy, to name just a few. Amazingly, each person who gives blood can improve, and save, the lives of up to three patients with a single donation. This is because each whole unit of blood can either be transfused as a single unit, or separated into three components and transfused to treat specific needs.

The Red Cross is not only the steward of the state's blood supply. Hematology-oncology physicians and their patients in Connecticut look to the Red Cross to perform a variety of state-of-the-art molecular testing on human leukocyte antigens (HLA). The HLA lab tests for related and unrelated bone marrow transplantation for Yale's transplant center, as well as for physicians and patients around the world.

In addition to bone marrow matching, the HLA lab performs platelet antibody workups for patients with a low platelet count, including newborns; conducts testing to aid in determining a patient's predisposition to a particular disease; and works closely with the Red Cross' special collections apheresis department to find particular donor platelet matches when a patient's needs demand it.

Health and Safety Services

Every year, the Charter Oak Chapter teaches more than 75,000 Connecticut residents how to help others in an emergency. People who have gone through Red Cross training know what to do when a family member, colleague or neighbor is in distress. The Red Cross offers more than two dozen different courses to businesses and

PHOTO/CAROLYN CARLSON

individuals and is constantly working to respond to the health and safety concerns of those who live, work or attend school locally by offering new and innovative programs. There are many different ways to obtain Red Cross training. Curriculums may differ, but every course taught helps Connecticut residents to be more confident and skilled when going to the aid of others.

Armed Forces Emergency

The Charter Oak Chapter serves as a local link to a worldwide communications network that connects military families with one another during times of separation. Red Cross caseworkers are on call 24 hours a day to ensure that messages regarding family emergencies, births, sicknesses or deaths are communicated promptly. This free service provides military personnel and their commanders with fast, reliable information to help them make decisions about emergency leave, deferment, compassionate reassignment and dependency discharge.

Volunteer Services

None of what the Red Cross does would be possible without the amazing devotion and hard work of its volunteer force, which is 3,000 people strong at the Charter Oak Chapter. Every day and night, Red Cross volunteers are donating their time and talents, lending professional support in offices, serving on boards and departmental committees, responding to late night fires, teaching CPR and first aid and so much more. They truly are the backbone of the organization. Their commitment to service enables the Red Cross to prevent, prepare for and respond to emergencies, and be a vital source of strength and compassion in its communities.

CHARTER OAK CHAPTER DISASTER VOLUNTEERS WORK ALONGSIDE LOCAL FIREFIGHTERS AT THE SCENE OF A BLAZE ON A CHILLY MARCH AFTERNOON. THE CHARTER OAK CHAPTER RESPONDS TO MORE THAN 250 FIRES EACH YEAR.

COPACO CENTER

It's a classic American success story: A Russian immigrant leaves his homeland and travels to America to make a better life. That's the tale of Kalman Bercowetz, who came to Connecticut in 1909 and bought hundreds of acres of land in the countryside, where Copaco Center stands today.

Photo/Steve Laschever

Kalman Bercowetz's descendents gather on the site of his original farm: (seated) Israel and Rhoda Rosenthal; (standing from left) Herman and Cynthia Bercowetz, and Paul Klopp and Bonnie Bercowetz

Today, 95 years later, Bercowetz's children and grandchildren have built upon his dream and have made Copaco Center into one of the state's most successful and fastest-growing shopping centers.

Despite the nation's tough retail economy in recent years, Copaco Center, which is located at 335 Cottage Grove Road in Bloomfield, is thriving and expanding like never before. Just minutes from Hartford and the intersection of I-91 and I-84, it is the site of more than 30 national and regionally owned stores, including Lowe's, Super Stop & Shop, and a brand new Burlington Coat Factory.

"In the past few years, the approval and construction of new retail space has doubled Copaco Center's lease capacity size to a total of 450,000 square feet," explains Bonnie S. Bercowetz, president of the Connecticut Packing Co. Inc., the family-owned business that owns and manages the shopping center in the same location where it started. The granddaughter of Kalman Bercowetz, she is the first female president in the company's history.

Copaco Center's expansion includes the airy, family-owned Copaco Liquors, which features 11,000 square feet of space, including a custom-designed temperature- and humidity-controlled wine room. The store's wine expert manages special wine tastings and dinners, wine classes, individual consultations and other activities to help customers discover wines best-suited to their individual tastes and budgets. The original Copaco liquor store was added to the center in 1972 when the previously "dry" Bloomfield first allowed the sale of alcohol.

Bonnie Bercowetz grew up in the family business, hearing about day-to-day business operations at the dinner table from her grandfather, father and uncles. She knew that during the Great Depression, years after he purchased the land, Kalman Bercowetz built a small meat packing plant called Connecticut Packing Co. Inc. on his Bloomfield farm as a way to provide jobs for his two sons, Herman and Irving. In 1947, they were joined by their brother-in-law, Israel Rosenthal. They steadily developed the Copaco property, adding a small grocery store, fruit and vegetable stand, and the original Mr. Frankee hot dog stand in the early 1950s.

By 1966, those businesses had grown into Copaco Supermarket on Cottage Grove Road, one of the largest supermarkets in the Northeast at that time, and the retail hub for one of Connecticut's faster-

PHOTO/STEVE ADAMS

growing communities. The complex later expanded to 265,000 square feet between 1972 and 1999.

In 1995, Copaco Center underwent a total renovation, adding new retailers to its thriving center. In April 2000, a 68,000-square-foot Super Stop & Shop opened as an anchor of the plaza and CVS Pharmacy built a freestanding 10,880-square-foot building with a drive-through window, only steps away from its previous site. Today, national chains, including Avenue, Boston Market and Dunkin Donuts, stand beside local businesses. For example, Battison's Cleaners and Bloomfield Opticians, the oldest tenants, are both family-owned and operated businesses that have been located in Copaco Center since the 1960s. An 81,000-square-foot Burlington Coat Factory opened late in 2004, as did the new Lowe's. Copaco Center's newest plans call for the completion of the final phase of its 450,000 square feet of retail space by 2007.

Although President Bonnie Bercowetz's father, Irving, passed away in 2002, his two partners still serve as corporate officers of the company: Herman Bercowetz as vice president and Israel Rosenthal as secretary. Paul Klopp, her husband, serves as director of operations and has been in charge of constructing and executing the master plan and sits on the company's board of directors. Her cousin, Alan Rosenthal, is assistant manager of Copaco Liquors. Other third generation members of the three original families serve as board members: Linda Einhorn, Donald Bercowetz and Daniel Rosenthal. Nearly all of the family members still reside in Bloomfield.

"Copaco Center is growing in exciting new areas because we know that to stay competitive, we must continue to reinvent ourselves," says Bonnie Bercowetz. "Our family is always looking for ways to stand out and be just a little different from the cookie-cutter, corporate shopping center owners."

Kalman Bercowetz would be proud.

COPACO CENTER'S PRESIDENT BONNIE BERCOWETZ AND DIRECTOR OF OPERATIONS PAUL KLOPP IN FRONT OF THEIR SHOPPING CENTER'S NEWEST ADDITION, BURLINGTON COAT FACTORY

GRIFFIN LAND

Griffin Land is one of the largest private property owners and developers in the region with approximately 4,000 acres in the Connecticut River Valley.

GRIFFIN CENTER OFFERS A DIVERSITY OF CLASS A OFFICE, FLEX AND DEVELOPMENT LAND PROPERTIES WITHIN A BEAUTIFULLY LANDSCAPED 600-ACRE BUSINESS PARK.

Griffin Land is the real estate division of Griffin Land & Nurseries Inc., a NASDAQ company (GRIF). Griffin's current real estate business includes the ownership, development and management of commercial and industrial properties, and the development of residential subdivisions on real estate it owns in Connecticut and Massachusetts.

Griffin is the award-winning developer of more than two million square feet of commercial and industrial space in the Hartford/Springfield corridor. Two of Griffin's largest business parks are Griffin Center in Windsor and Bloomfield and the New England Tradeport, which spans Windsor and East Granby.

A History of High Quality Speculative Development

Griffin Land today is an expansion of what was previously the real estate operation of Culbro Corporation, whose predecessors had grown tobacco in the Hartford area since 1910. Eight decades later, in 1997, assets of the tobacco-oriented Culbro Corporation were separated and the newly formed Griffin Land & Nurseries, with Culbro's non-tobacco interests, was spun off.

Efforts of Griffin Land and its predecessor, both of which have been centered on high-quality, long-term speculative development, began with the early development of Griffin Center in the 1970s, and the New England Tradeport and early residential developments in the 1980s. The company continues to be focused on these goals today as Griffin Land accelerates an already aggressive program of speculative and build-to-suit construction. Since 1997, Griffin Land has successfully built and leased eight buildings totaling more than 750,000 square feet.

Griffin Center: A Bright Light

Griffin Center, comprised of Griffin Office Center and Griffin Center South, is a 600-acre master-planned business park located on the Bloomfield/Windsor town line. Conceived more than three decades ago, Griffin Center is located three miles from Interstate 91, with easy access to New York, Hartford, Northern New England and Bradley International Airport. The park integrates high-quality, environmentally sensitive business facilities with scenic natural surroundings in an ideal location for prime office facilities. It is truly one of Greater Hartford's bright lights.

To date, more than 2,000 employees work in nearly 2 million square feet of space in Griffin Center. Among the many high-profile businesses and services to be sited here are ALSTOM, CIGNA, The Hartford Financial Services Group, Johnson Controls, Ohio Casualty, Raytel Medical, TRC Environmental, the United States Postal Service and Wells Fargo.

Griffin Land continues to nurture this highly regarded development. The company owns significant acreage within the park that can support hundreds of thousands of additional square feet of office development.

New England Tradeport: Engine Powering Regional Business Growth

The New England Tradeport, a 600-acre industrial business park strategically located near Interstate 91 in the towns of Windsor and East Granby, is a major resource for the industrial and economic development of the area.

Because of its proximity to Bradley International Airport, a rapidly growing passenger and cargo transport hub, and its easy access to I-91, New England Tradeport has emerged as an "address for success," both as a magnet for some of the top companies in America and as an economic engine that powers regional business growth. Domestic and international businesses within the park have included Domino's Pizza, FedEx, Excel, Matheson, Eaton/Cutler-Hammer, The Hartford Financial Services Group, Pepsi Cola, Pitney Bowes and Westinghouse Electric Co.

Economic development figures underscore the success story that the New England Tradeport represents. There are more than 1,000 employees in Tradeport who add significant revenue to the region's economy. Growth is projected to accelerate, due to the 400+ acres of undeveloped land within the park, which can support the development of millions of additional square feet of industrial space and potentially create a location for thousands of additional jobs.

Residential Master Planning

Griffin Land is also a skilled master planner of residential communities. Its first notable project began in the early 1990s with the development of the award-winning Walden Woods master-planned community, which consists of 336 units of single and attached residences. As of late 2004, Griffin has applications pending for a 360-acre development in Simsbury known as Meadowood, and in Suffield, Griffin has begun the development of a 50-lot neighborhood, known as Stratton Farms. With more than a thousand acres of land that is viable for residential development, Griffin intends to be a neighborhood developer of the highest quality for years to come.

SummerWind: Breath of Fresh Air

Complementing its business focus, Griffin Land also strongly supports the arts in the Greater Hartford area. In 2000, the firm was especially proud to become a founding sponsor of the exciting SummerWind Performing Arts Center, a world-class, outdoor amphitheater at Griffin Center.

Now known as the ADVO SummerWind Performing Arts Center, New England's newest venue for the performing arts, this exciting facility has taken a prominent place in the region and the arts world as a premiere amphitheater and host to world-class performing arts talent. The center sits on 10 beautiful acres made available by Griffin Land & Nurseries Inc. Its inaugural season in 2002 saw a stellar arts calendar of 12 concerts, ranging from classical, jazz, and rhythm and blues to ethnic, folk and American music.

Commitment to Excellence

As a real estate owner, developer and manager, Griffin Land has forged a reputation for setting and adhering to the highest standards. The construction of high-quality buildings that retain their value and are accommodating to tenant needs is the cornerstone of the company's long-term ownership philosophy.

This philosophy has borne fruit. Griffin tenants show a tendency to stay and grow within the Griffin Land portfolio. Griffin Land enjoys excellent relationships with both the municipalities in which it owns

and develops commercial and industrial property, and the commercial building and brokerage communities in the construction and leasing of much of its office and industrial space.

Griffin Land's strategic mission and vision – to own, operate, construct and manage office and industrial properties of the highest quality – will sustain and enhance the company's stature among the state's top private landlord/developers and as one of the state's most respected and admired corporate citizens.

"All of Griffin's projects reflect our company's commitment to quality and long-term ownership," according to Frederick M. Danziger, president and CEO of Griffin Land. "It is in this manner that we intend to continue developing our extensive land holdings for the years to come."

THE 600-ACRE NEW ENGLAND TRADEPORT INDUSTRIAL BUSINESS PARK IS WITHIN CLOSE PROXIMITY TO BRADLEY INTERNATIONAL AIRPORT AND THE INTERSTATE HIGHWAY SYSTEM.

ALSTOM

ALSTOM is a world-leading solutions provider of power generation services and equipment as well as a global builder of ships and trains.

ENGINEERS AND TECHNICIANS WORK IN ALSTOM'S WORLD RENOWNED POWER RESEARCH FACILITIES FOCUSING ON WAYS TO IMPROVE THE EFFICIENCY AND PERFORMANCE OF ALL TYPES OF POWER GENERATING SYSTEMS AND DEVELOPING ENVIRONMENTALLY RESPONSIBLE IDEAS FOR THE POWER INDUSTRY.

As an international corporation, ALSTOM is dedicated to diversity and greatly values the inclusion of new ideas and viewpoints. The corporation is committed to providing innovation and excellence in solving infrastructure problems for industry through the strength of its technology and the capabilities, experience and diversity of its employees. A few of the company's notable accomplishments include: building the 150,000-ton Queen Mary 2, the world's largest cruise ship; building power plants that are responsible for 20 percent of the world's total installed capacity in power generation; and supplying trains and locomotives that run on six continents, including the Acela high-speed locomotives that whisk passengers between Boston and Washington, D.C.

ALSTOM's U.S. headquarters are located in Windsor. The company's roots in the United States include businesses that were formerly part of Combustion Engineering, a company founded in New York City in 1912. The company moved its headquarters to Day Hill Road in Windsor in 1960. The company then became a wholly owned subsidiary of Asea Brown Boveri Inc. (ABB) in 1990. ABB ALSTOM Power was formed as a joint venture between ALSTOM and ABB in 1999, and in 2000, ALSTOM acquired the ABB interest in the joint venture.

ALSTOM's Research & Development facilities, located in Windsor, provide a constant flow of fresh ideas and new products to the power industry, enabling the company's customers to meet energy demands utilizing the best available environmental control technologies. The Windsor operation specializes in combustion research, environmental control systems, electronics and electrical systems, materials and water chemistry, and process engineering and design with a daily focus on ways to improve the efficiency and performance of all types of power generating systems – from coal, oil and natural gas to biomass.

The company aims to provide the most economical and environmentally friendly solutions to keep plants profitable and competitive. It is continually developing new service products to support its customers' success, enhancing power plant maintenance and management, and improving plant and component performance. ALSTOM is a world leader in environmental equipment including sulfur dioxide removal, nitrogen oxide reduction, and particulate control. Coal combustion products developed in Windsor are used in 19 of the top 20 cleanest coal-fired units in the U.S., determined by the U.S. Environmental Protection Agency.

As the company has grown and changed, so has the town where it makes its home. When ALSTOM relocated to Windsor from New York City, the town was dominated by two pursuits: tobacco farming and brick making. The last brickyard disappeared in the 1960s, but tobacco is still grown on land near the ALSTOM campus. Windsor's industrial base now encompasses a wide range of products and services. The company's proximity to Interstate 91 and Bradley International

tributions and volunteers. The company also supports "Everybody Wins! CT," a reading and mentoring program at Clover Street Elementary School in Windsor.

ALSTOM's volunteers lend their expertise to the Connecticut Pre-Engineering Program, a program for fifth graders at Mark Twain Elementary School in Hartford, aimed to help these young people discover the powers of mathematics, science and engineering. Red Cross blood drives are held on the campus and are well supported by employees.

Through its innovative ideas and strong volunteer efforts, ALSTOM has positioned itself as a leader in the local community. On a global scale, the company is committed to finding new ways to make the best use of available energy supplies and be the first company people think of when they need power generation services and equipment.

The president of ALSTOM's U.S. operations, Tim Curran, is a longtime resident of the Greater Hartford area.

Airport provides easy access for transportation to locations around the world.

There are more than 1,000 ALSTOM employees in Greater Hartford and 5,500 ALSTOM employees in the United States. For many years, ALSTOM played a large part in Windsor's annual festival, the Shad Derby. The United Way is supported through employee charitable giving and volunteer work on the Day of Caring each year, when ALSTOM employees pair with the Windsor Police Explorers. It supports the Special Olympics with company con-

ALSTOM's U.S. HEADQUARTERS IN WINDSOR. AN INTERNATIONAL, MULTICULTURAL ORGANIZATION, ALSTOM HAS MORE THAN 40,000 EMPLOYEES IN 70 COUNTRIES.

THE SAWYER SCHOOL

Located in downtown Hartford, The Sawyer School provides students with the opportunity to train as medical and business office assistants, thus filling the employment needs of local firms while improving the quality of the city's work force.

A Sawyer instructor conducts a review session to help students in the medical program prepare for an important exam.

The school has an average annual enrollment of 350 students, of which 90 percent are Hartford residents. The vast majority of Sawyer graduates find employment in the Greater Hartford area.

The Sawyer School offers two 13-month programs designed to prepare students for business and medical careers. The medical assistant/secretary program provides graduates with the knowledge and skills needed to begin a career in medical offices, hospitals and walk-in clinics. In the office information systems program, students learn computer skills, customer service techniques, and accounting and business management skills which help them qualify for positions in both large and small business firms, including local insurance companies.

The Sawyer School was founded in downtown Los Angeles in 1916 and grew to become a national franchise, with branches predominantly in the Los Angeles area and Pennsylvania. In 1975, Rhode Island-based Academic Enterprises purchased The Sawyer School's two campuses in that state with plans for expansion. In 1990, Pelham Educational Group formed in Connecticut and opened the current schools in Hartford and Hamden. In 1999, Academic Enterprises purchased the Butler Business School, which had been established in Bridgeport for more than a century. Today, all five schools are owned and operated by The Sawyer School.

In 2002, the Sawyer School introduced an ability-to-benefit (ATB) program allowing students without a high school diploma to participate in the medical or business programs. The school also assists ATB students in attaining their high school diploma free of charge.

The Sawyer School is accredited by the Accrediting Council for Independent Colleges and Schools and is approved to provide training services to government-funded programs. The school is a member of the National Business Educators Association, the National Association of Professional Financial Aid Administrators and the Connecticut Business Educators Association.

In addition to training qualified employees, The Sawyer School believes it is important to contribute something more to the Hartford community, and therefore hosts regular in-house blood drives to benefit the American Red Cross.

As Hartford moves into the future, The Sawyer School takes pride in its mission to always be aware of employers' needs, to create relevant curricula, and to enhance the abilities of students enrolled by improving their quality of life through career education.

UCONN SCHOOL OF BUSINESS

The University of Connecticut founded its School of Business in Storrs in 1941, during the throes of the Second World War.

When the university established Connecticut's first evening master of business administration program in 1957, its classrooms were filled with veterans of the Korean Conflict and World War II attending school with GI Bill education benefits.

In 1958, UConn's School of Business, including its MBA program, received accreditation from the prestigious AACSB International (Association to Advance Collegiate Schools of Business) – a designation the school holds to this day. Several periods of growth led the MBA program to expand to Hartford, Stamford and Waterbury – and diversify its student body.

The full-time, part-time and executive MBA students of today are a critical element of Connecticut's workforce. Students come from a wide range of professional disciplines and educational backgrounds to acquire the managerial and creative problem-solving skills needed to succeed in business.

In August 2004, a new chapter in the school's history was written with the relocation of the school's metro Hartford MBA programs to downtown, along with the launch of its latest experiential learning initiative, the SS&C Technologies Financial Accelerator, at 100 Constitution Plaza. This move to downtown Hartford brought the School of Business to the heart of Connecticut's Insurance and Financial Services Industry Cluster.

At the SS&C Technologies Financial Accelerator, both graduate and undergraduate students work with faculty and business executives to develop innovative solutions to real problems facing the financial services industry, further differentiating the learning experience students have at the UConn School of Business. Using technology as an enabler, students, faculty and the school's business partners investigate alternative markets and trader support tools, study insider trading identification and control, review alternative auction market mechanisms, design financial product bundling alternatives that enhance competitive advantage, evaluate emerging technologies, and create specialized algorithms and business processes that improve efficiency, reduce costs and

THE UCONN SCHOOL OF BUSINESS GRADUATE LEARNING CENTER IN DOWNTOWN HARTFORD (ABOVE).

UCONN MBA STUDENTS STUDY IN TECHNOLOGICALLY ADVANCED LEARNING LABORATORIES (TOP RIGHT).

increase revenues of firms in the industry.

The short and long-term benefits of the Financial Accelerator to students, faculty and business partners are real and significant. It represents a real-world lab for the faculty's ground-breaking research. Business partners take away innovative solutions to current market challenges that have been put to the test using real market data and they have access to a pipeline of top talent that will evolve into their next generation of leadership. UConn students work in an environment that leverages the traditional with experiential learning in their quest to capture one of the best business educations available anywhere.

Along with the Financial Accelerator, UConn's School of Business hosts over a dozen centers and institutes that serve as living learning laboratories for its students, producing real results for affiliated partners. These include *edgelab* (sm), the school's groundbreaking partnership with General Electric, the ING Center for Financial Services, and the Center for Real Estate and Urban Economic Studies. These and more are all part of a cutting-edge business curriculum that immerses students in real-life problems.

The University of Connecticut School of Business and its innovative experiential learning programs continues to live its mission – preparing leaders who implement creative solutions to complex business problems through people and technology.

UNITED TECHNOLOGIES CORPORATION

Few companies can change the world. United Technologies Corporation (UTC) is one of those few. The seven global businesses of UTC create new possibilities on every continent, in nearly every corner of our lives.

PHOTO/FRED GAYLOR

UTC, WHICH OPERATES IN MORE THAN 180 COUNTRIES, HAS ITS HEADQUARTERS IN THE "GOLD BUILDING," 1 FINANCIAL PLAZA, IN DOWNTOWN HARTFORD.

*I*ts success has a strong foundation: superb technical knowledge, critical mass and a proven commitment to quality, efficiency, productivity and values. UTC's employees put these resources to work daily, building not only better solutions but also the basis for better lives, planet-wide.

UTC operates in more than 180 countries, with more than 200,000 employees worldwide. It is headquartered in Hartford, and the headquarters of all its business units are in Connecticut, six of them in Greater Hartford.

Although parts of the company – notably Chubb and Otis – originated in the 19th century, UTC dates its official founding to 1929 when Pratt & Whitney Aircraft joined United Aircraft & Transport Corp. The name United Technologies Corporation was chosen by the company in 1975 "to connote the breadth of its products, markets and activities."

UTC's businesses were founded on great ideas that have made them leaders in their industries.

Carrier

Carrier is the world's largest company providing heating, ventilating, air conditioning and refrigeration solutions, with operations in 172 countries. Each day around the world, a Carrier unit is shipped every four seconds and installed every eight seconds. Carrier products serve the Sistine Chapel, George Washington's Mount Vernon mansion, Yale University's rare book library, the Great Hall of the People in Beijing, the Queen Mary 2 and the Tate Modern Gallery in London, in addition to countless homes, buildings and refrigerated transportation systems worldwide.

Carrier is an environmental leader and was the first air conditioning manufacturer to provide chlorine-free alternative refrigerants in its entire product line, from residential to large commercial applications.

Chubb

A world leader in fire safety and security services founded in 1818, Chubb joined UTC in 2003. Chubb combines innovative security solutions and customer service to provide products and services to more than a million customers worldwide.

In the fire safety industry, Chubb designs, installs and services fire detection, fixed suppression and portable systems. In the electronic security industry, Chubb designs, integrates, installs and services intruder alarms, access control systems and video surveillance systems. Chubb also provides monitoring, response and guarding services to complement both the fire safety and electronic security businesses.

Hamilton Sundstrand

Hamilton Sundstrand serves both aerospace and industrial markets. Its aviation products include engine and environmental control systems, flight controls, auxiliary power units, and many other systems and components for both commercial and military markets. It's a leading supplier for Boeing's new 7E7 Dreamliner aircraft. Hamilton Sundstrand also is prime contractor for NASA's space suit/life support system.

Hamilton Sundstrand's industrial products include power transmission equipment, metering pumps and systems, compressors, pumps, and blowers.

Otis

The most global of UTC's businesses is Otis. Its products are sold worldwide; it maintains manufacturing facilities in the Americas, Europe and Asia, and has engineering and testing centers in the United States, Japan, China, Korea, Italy, France, Germany and Spain. Otis technicians provide maintenance and repair services to 1.4 million elevators and escalators in nearly every country in the world.

Otis' recent technological innovations include its Gen2™ elevator, based on the first major breakthrough in lifting technology in nearly 150 years. Gen2 uses flat, coated steel belts instead of standard steel cables. Otis' NextStep™ escalator makes a giant leap forward in safety by combining the step with the protective side disk, eliminating the gap between the moving step riser and the side.

In addition to its well-known elevators and escalators, Otis also makes, installs and services moving walkways and other horizontal transportation systems.

Pratt & Whitney

Pratt & Whitney is a pioneer in flight and technology. Over the years it has patented thousands of aerospace innovations, from heat-resistant coatings to aerodynamic fan blades – technologies that make air travel more cost-effective and more dependable.

Pratt & Whitney engines power many of the world's leading commercial airlines, and the company has long-term maintenance agreements with airlines and other customers as part of its growing after-market business.

Its military engines power the Air Force's front-line fighters of today – the F-15 and F-16 – and its F119 and F135 engines will power the front-line fighters of the future – the F-22 Raptor and Joint Strike Fighter. Pratt & Whitney rocket engines send payloads into orbit, and its gas turbines are used to generate electricity on Earth.

Sikorsky

All branches of the U.S. armed forces, along with military services and commercial operators in more than 40 nations, use Sikorsky helicopters. More than 2,000 Sikorsky H-60 Black Hawk and H-60 variants are flown by all five U.S. military departments. More than 600 international S-70 helicopter variants, including Seahawk naval derivatives, serve 25 international customers.

Sikorsky is leading the industry team that created the S-92 helicopter, a versatile craft that can carry passengers or cargo or be used for search and rescue missions.

UTC Power

UTC Power is a world leader in fuel cell production and innovative on-site power delivery systems. UTC Power and its UTC Fuel Cells unit also have adapted fuel cell technology to power buses and automobiles with near-zero environmental impact.

While each business unit has its own research and development capabilities, much of UTC's innovative research takes shape at the United Technologies Research Center in East Hartford. Its engineers and scientists have proven themselves world leaders in technologies ranging from fluid dynamics to advanced materials.

As UTC's businesses change our world, the company and its employees are working together to ensure the planet is a better place for us and the generations that follow.

Continued on next page

CARRIER

CHUBB

HAMILTON SUNDSTRAND

OTIS

PRATT & WHITNEY

SIKORSKY

UTC POWER

UNITED TECHNOLOGIES CORPORATION

Continued from previous page

PHOTO/DEREK DUDEK

THE INNOVATIVE EMPLOYEE SCHOLAR PROGRAM HAS PROVIDED MORE THAN $430 MILLION IN COLLEGE COSTS AND STOCK AWARDS TO UTC EMPLOYEE GRADUATES.

UTC is a global company committed to social responsibility. Over the last 80 years, it has been a mainstay of Greater Hartford. UTC continues its historical civic commitment by encouraging employees to become involved in their communities.

UTC strongly believes that volunteerism brings about significant change, large and small, in the world. Each year in Greater Hartford, UTC contributes more than $6 million, and employees donate more than 50,000 hours to more than 80 organizations and programs focused on education, human services, arts and culture, and the environment. UTC also matches, dollar for dollar, more than a quarter of a million dollars in contributions that employees make to Connecticut organizations annually.

Throughout the year, UTC and its employees make a major contribution to the community. During March and April, engineers from UTC's business units team with high school students to build robots for the FIRST Robotics competition. FIRST (For Inspiration and Recognition of Science and Technology) is a national sports-like competition aimed at sparking student interest in science, engineering and technology.

Since 1999, UTC has contributed more than $1.4 million to sponsor the FIRST New England regional competition, which brings

together some 35 teams from across the region for a three-day contest. FIRST represents more than 60 percent of UTC's total volunteer hours nationally. Each year, team-member volunteers, student mentors and regional volunteers donate, on average, more than 27,000 hours.

The arts are another priority. Over the past decade, UTC and its employees have contributed more than $15 million to supporting the arts locally and nationally. Each year, UTC and its employees are significant contributors to the United Arts Campaign of the Greater Hartford Arts Council, which raises money on behalf of more than 100 organizations in the area. More than 20 UTC executives volunteer to serve on boards of arts and cultural organizations.

Enthusiastic UTC volunteers make possible another high-profile community event: the Special Olympics Connecticut Summer Games. In June, more than 1,000 UTC volunteers donate their time to organize and supervise two days of track and field events for the Summer Games. This commitment dates back to 1977 and is an important part of UTC's community traditions.

Every fall, UTC and its employees typically give more to the United Way of the Capital Area than any other organization. With a corporate donation and a workplace campaign, UTC and its employees contribute more than $7 million to the United Way annually, nearly 30 percent of the campaign's total.

In October, nearly 400 UTC employees volunteer at, or run in, the United Technologies Greater Hartford Marathon, which draws more than 6,000 participants from all over the world. This event, which raises funds for the Connecticut Children's Medical Center, provides important lessons in health, endurance and discipline.

Each December, UTC's holiday gift to Greater Hartford is United Technologies Symphony on Ice®, a free skating and music performance that collects toys for the U.S. Marines' Toys for Tots program, which benefits less-fortunate children during the holidays. Admission to the event is free with the donation of a toy. Since 1980, nearly 9,000 UTC volunteers have helped collect approximately 300,000 toys for the Toys for Tots program.

UTC employees are eager volunteers. "When you are out in the community, doing the volunteer work, you can see gratification right on the person's face. It makes you feel a little bit more excited to get out there and do it again," says rJo Winch, a UTC employee and active community volunteer.

UTC extends its corporate citizenship to the natural environment, as well as cultural and community institutions. UTC is working toward a sustainable future, striving to consider social, economic and environmental effects when making business decisions: "triple bottom line" thinking that ultimately preserves resources and minimizes environmental impact.

Over the last decade, UTC has reduced its air emissions by 90 percent and its hazardous waste emissions by 85 percent. UTC has an impressive portfolio of environmentally friendly products across its business units, ranging from UTC Power's fuel cell power for cars, which produces electricity without environmentally harmful emissions, to the world's first zero-volatile organic compound paint coating that Sikorsky uses on helicopters to reduce air emissions.

In Connecticut, UTC maintains a commitment to environmental sustainability by supporting the Connecticut chapter of the Nature Conservancy, which works to promote biodiversity and protect the natural habitat of the state's rarest and most threatened plants, animals and natural communities. UTC also supports the Trust for Public Land, which works to preserve the Connecticut River watershed, New England's largest river ecosystem.

UTC's social responsibility begins with its employees. The foundation of UTC's future is a talented, well-educated work force. In 1996, UTC Chairman and Chief Executive Officer George David introduced the Employee Scholar Program, a unique program that pays for college tuition, books and fees up front, doesn't require that study be related to an employee's job, and awards a substantial gift of UTC stock when the

employee graduates. The goal, as David says, is "the best educated work force on the planet."

Since the program began, UTC has spent more than $430 million on college costs and stock awards.

Not surprisingly, employees are enthusiastic about the Employee Scholar Program. "I came from a broken family and we didn't have the available financial resources to go to college. It was a wonderful opportunity for me to get into a company with such extraordinary educational benefits," says David Osowiski, an employee at UTC's Corporate Learning and Development Center. He's one of more than 15,000 UTC employees who've received a degree

because of the Employee Scholar Program.

"It says a lot about a company when they provide education to all employees, not just a select few," he says.

UTC's employees, its communities and its customers all benefit from the corporation's commitments to performance, pioneering innovation, personal development, social responsibility and shareowner value.

PHOTO/FRED GAYLOR

UTC EMPLOYEES ARE EAGER VOLUNTEERS IN THEIR COMMUNITIES. NATASHA ROUNTREE IS ONE OF SCORES OF UTC EMPLOYEES WHO ANNUALLY PERFORM WORK FOR NONPROFIT ORGANIZATIONS AS PART OF THE UNITED WAY DAY OF CARING.

VAN ZELM HEYWOOD & SHADFORD INC.

Founded in 1930 by Henri B. van Zelm while our nation was in the depths of the Great Depression, van Zelm Heywood & Shadford Inc. managed not only to surmount initial economic hardship, but has also been able to achieve consistent growth in the ensuing years.

PHOTO/JENEEN M. WUNDER

(ABOVE) HARTFORD HOSPITAL C.O.R.E.

RECIPIENT OF THE NATIONAL 2002 INTEGRATOR AWARD, THE COMPLEX, FOUR-STORY ADDITION AUGMENTS HARTFORD HOSPITAL'S CENTRAL STERILE, EMERGENCY, OPERATING, AND RADIOLOGY DEPARTMENTS.

(RIGHT) UNIVERSITY OF CONNECTICUT LAW LIBRARY

LOCATED IN HARTFORD'S WEST END, THE NEW LAW LIBRARY IS DESIGNED TO BLEND PERFECTLY WITH THE GOTHIC ARCHITECTURE OF THE SURROUNDING HISTORIC BUILDINGS. VAN ZELM DESIGNED THE BUILDING SYSTEMS THAT PROVIDE COMFORT AND SAFETY FOR THIS BEAUTIFUL ADDITION TO THE UNIVERSITY OF CONNECTICUT LAW SCHOOL CAMPUS.

*I*n 2005, as van Zelm celebrates its 75th anniversary, it looks back with pride on a portfolio of notable projects that have earned the firm a place of distinction in the world of engineering design.

Henri van Zelm, a Dartmouth College and Pratt Institute graduate, was a man of high principles and determination who believed that client satisfaction and quality design are essential to successful growth and repeat client business. The third and fourth generations of principals and staff at the mechanical and electrical engineering design firm of van Zelm Heywood & Shadford Inc. continue to embrace that culture and philosophy today.

Today, the 82-person firm completes designs for more than $60 million worth of mechanical and electrical construction costs annually. The company works internationally as well as domestically and has recently designed projects in Poland and Mexico. Its present day success is due, in part, to the mutually supportive and collaborative relationships van Zelm has enjoyed with its clients, in addition to the backing and encouragement the firm has found in its home state of Connecticut.

The firm's designs are responsive to each client's individual project needs. It excels in allowing its engineers and designers the freedom to use their talent and creativity in developing designs under the guidance and mentoring of those responsible for overall project management. The standard of education is high for van Zelm's staff to ensure that clients are provided with the best designs possible. Specialists are trained in about 20 areas, including sustainable design, commissioning, indoor air quality, telecommunications systems, lighting systems,

PHOTO/JENEEN M. WUNDER

plumbing systems, fire protection systems, emergency and standby generation, integrated control design, and medium and low voltage distribution systems. The firm's technical expertise runs deep; senior staff members even develop and teach engineering courses that are open to the public, as well as to firm members, through a unique partnership with Capital Community College.

In the early 1960s, van Zelm designed all of the mechanical and electrical systems for the landmark Jefferson National Expansion Memorial, commonly known as the St. Louis Arch. In one project alone in the mid-1980s, van Zelm provided the MEP/FP design for two million square feet of renovations, done in more than 30 phases, at the Aetna Life & Casualty Insurance Company's home office facility in Hartford.

In 2002, the firm completed an intricate and challenging four-story addition for the central sterile, emergency, operating and radiology departments at Hartford Hospital. The firm also boasts an extensive list of classroom, laboratory, athletic, library and dormitory projects at academic institutions including the University of Connecticut, Trinity College, Wesleyan University, Yale University, Smith College, Cornell University and Harvard University. The firm has also provided ongoing design services to clients in Connecticut's distinguished pharmaceutical and biotech sectors. In addition, van Zelm is currently completing the new Musculoskeletal Center at the University of Connecticut Health Center, and was involved in the initial planning for Front Street at Adriaen's Landing.

Over the years, the firm's projects have garnered dozens of design awards. In Hartford, some of these include The Bushnell Center for the Performing Arts' Belding Theater, Capital Community College, The Learning Corridor, The Hartford Insurance Company, Fleet Bank's Corporate Services Center, and Southern New England Telecommunications Corp. (now SBC).

The company's award-winning work spreads well beyond the capital city. It has also earned awards for, among others, projects at the Warner Theater in Torrington, the Learning Resource and Technology Center at Manchester Community College, Miss Porter's School in Farmington, the Yale University Boyer Center for Molecular Medicine in New Haven, and the Harry A. Gampel Pavilion and Wolf-Zackin Natatorium in Storrs.

Even with an increasingly global clientele – about 90 percent of which is repeat clients – van Zelm Heywood & Shadford Inc. management and staff recognize the importance of local philanthropy, nurturing a tradition of charitable contributions and making a concerted effort to support engineering education in the state. For example, the van Zelm Heywood & Shadford Inc. Scholarship has been established at the University of Hartford to assist students at the College of Engineering, Technology and Architecture. The firm also participates in, and actively supports, the ACE Mentor Program of Connecticut and employs college engineering students whenever possible. It also supports the March of Dimes, an organization that has been working since 1938 to ensure that each generation of children has a healthy start in life, as well as other charitable organizations.

A key to the company's success over the past 75 years is its commitment to continuous quality improvement. Staff members recognize there is quality "in-fact" and quality "perceived." Quality in-fact is achieved by hiring the best staff, providing them with

PHOTO/ROBERT BENSON

ongoing training and education, and submitting their work to a rigorous design review process. Clients, from whom the firm solicits input through written surveys and focus group meetings, determine perceived quality. The firm continually looks both inward and outward, fine tuning its strategic philosophy and changing to meet the demands of the times. This guiding philosophy, instituted by Henri B. van Zelm in 1930, has been reaffirmed, and has evolved throughout the firm's entire history.

Says Bob Hickey, the firm's president and CEO for the past 16 years, "When you can drive past a building and say 'We were a part of that,' it's a wonderful legacy."

PHOTO/JENEEN M. WUNDER

THE BUSHNELL CENTER FOR THE PERFORMING ARTS' BELDING THEATER

WINNER OF MULTIPLE DESIGN AND PROJECT TEAM AWARDS, THE NEW BELDING THEATER IS SITUATED NEXT TO HISTORIC MORTENSEN HALL. VAN ZELM IS PROUD TO PROVIDE ENGINEERING DESIGN AND CONSULTING SERVICES FOR THIS HARTFORD ICON.

THE LEARNING CORRIDOR

SPONSORED BY THE SINA GROUP IN THE CITY OF HARTFORD, THIS RECLAIMED AND REDEVELOPED NEIGHBORHOOD IS NOW HOME TO A UNIQUE REGIONAL CAMPUS THAT INCLUDES A MONTESSORI SCHOOL, MIDDLE SCHOOL, AND A SCIENCE & ARTS MAGNET SCHOOL. VAN ZELM WAS THE LEAD DESIGN ENGINEER FOR THIS NATIONALLY AWARD-WINNING CAMPUS THAT CONNECTS TRINITY COLLEGE WITH THE INSTITUTE OF LIVING AND HARTFORD HOSPITAL.

TRANTOLO & TRANTOLO LLC

Before the days of the 1938 flood, before the tragic 1944 fire at the Ringling Bros.' circus and before the Hartford Civic Center was even an idea, Trantolo & Trantolo was established in Hartford.

SITTING, VINCENT TRANTOLO. STANDING FROM LEFT, VINCENT DEANGELO, KEITH TRANTOLO AND SCOTT TRANTOLO.

This legal institution has long been a staple in Hartford's legal system. It was originally founded as the manifestation of the dedication, honor and commitment of Joseph Trantolo, Sr.

The law firm's roots reach back to 1938, when Joseph Trantolo saw people around him struggling because they could not afford adequate legal attention. He unmistakably recognized the social inequalities preventing people from getting what they deserved; legal assistance had unfairly become a privilege for only the wealthy. Joseph Trantolo, even at a young age, found himself committed to helping to defend and protect the people around him who were injured or unfairly treated and he began to help the citizens of Hartford.

In 1958, three long-time practitioners, Joseph Trantolo, Waldemar Lach and Edward Krawiecki, joined together to form a general practice law firm located at 750 Main St. The firm's deep dedication to the public quickly earned them a respected place within the Hartford community. These three men represented a history of distinguished service in Connecticut and throughout the nation. Individuals from this firm were central figures in the legal, civic and political organizations of their time, acting as trustees, officers and members of legal committees, judicial foundations, civic groups, charities and commissions.

Joseph Trantolo, Sr. was the director of Legal Services Inc., an organization founded to provide counsel to the indigent, the prosecutor at the Hartford Police Court from 1948-1949, and was nominated as a candidate for the state Senate. Waldemar Lach was a municipal court judge in Newington, and would later serve in California as a federal judge within the Social Security system. From 1953 to 1959, Edward Krawiecki lectured at UConn Law School and represented Bristol in the state House of Representatives. The union of their efforts and reputations resulted in the creation of a law firm that would prove to be successful for generations to come.

The attorneys of Trantolo & Trantolo have always been sincerely dedicated to their clients' success. Joseph Trantolo, Sr. knew, and passed onto his sons, that fighting for clients meant more than providing successful legal advice. It meant providing emotional support for families. It meant stepping outside traditional legal boundaries to provide meaningful, insightful and most importantly, effective support.

Upon joining their father, Vincent and Joe Jr. created the Connecticut Law Clinics of Trantolo & Trantolo in 1976. Joe Jr. and Vincent came from a background in which they were dedicated to social improvement, so the progression to follow in their father's footprints and provide passionate, professional legal representation was a natural one.

Joe Jr. often worked with police officers in Greater Hartford, providing essential legal advice. In 1999, Vincent co-founded the Hartford County Bar Foundation, a charitable organization whose purpose is to develop, promote, provide and/or support programs of an altruistic nature that benefit the homeless, hungry, sick, disabled, unemployed and/or other disadvantaged or needy persons. He was also a pioneer in groundbreaking media and marketing innovations, and impacted both the state and national legal communities. Vincent Trantolo was able to create an indelible brand name throughout the state by effectively challenging the traditional marketing methods of the legal system. He fought his way straight to the Connecticut Supreme Court in his bold efforts to confront the status quo and the antiquated marketing traditions within the practice of law.

Sixty-seven years after Joseph Trantolo, Sr. began providing legal assistance to Hartford's small communities, the firm, now led by Vincent Trantolo and Vincent DeAngelo, is still known as the personal injury law firm that does things differently. Vincent Trantolo is widely known by his friends, associates, family and clients as an advocate who will do whatever it takes to fight for those people who cannot fight for themselves. Every day, this family law firm is given the opportunity to have its clients become its friends. It is through this reality that the firm is able to prove just how honorable the legal profession can be.

Vincent Trantolo knows that accident victims and their families need more than legal knowledge; they need compassion. He says, "I firmly believe a lawyer should fight for you when you can't fight for yourself because without dedicated representation, injured people would be at the mercy of powerful insurance companies. I understand that it takes more than just knowledge of the law to win. It takes compassion for clients and their families and a sincere passion for

success." Trantolo & Trantolo is the community-focused law firm that is small enough to still dedicate its services to very poor clients, but is large enough to challenge the wealthiest and largest corporations.

Trantolo & Trantolo LLC is well known for its traditional practices of personal injury and medical malpractice suits, including wrongful death or misdiagnosis. The firm also specializes in mass tort and securities fraud litigation. It has been able to maintain a high level of personal attention and use an expert paralegal staff to help clients successfully meet their needs.

Today, as in the past, the firm focuses many of its efforts on community education, realizing that even though its members are proud of the work they do with people who are injured, it's the proactive work they do to prevent those injures that really inspires them. The firm works with local nursing homes to educate the elderly and their families about safe living. It works with local schools to educate families about "Stranger Danger" and bicycle safety. Trantolo & Trantolo's staff is committed to giving back to the society of which it is a part.

In 2004, as the third generation of Trantolo sons joins the firm, Keith and Scott, one reality remains at the forefront of its focus: it is committed to responding to the changing needs of the community. The Trantolo family recognizes the difficulties that come with being a part of a community that is growing increasingly competitive, as insurance companies and law firms grow stronger. In fact, they welcome the challenge. The firm has established a history of integrity, compassion, excellence and dedication to good old-fashioned hard work and success, and proudly carries this tradition into the future.

The compassion of the firm's members, coupled with expert legal knowledge, is what makes Trantolo & Trantolo a unique firm. In an industry where longevity and unwavering compassion are often the exception rather than the rule, Trantolo & Trantolo LLC has proven itself as a unique entity. With a special concentration in the area of negligence law, the firm has continued to grow and serve its community and clients for more than 65 years.

SITTING, CATHERINE TRANTOLO.

STANDING FROM LEFT,

JOSEPH TRANTOLO JR.,

VINCENT TRANTOLO AND

MARK TRANTOLO.

COX COMMUNICATIONS

It is hard to tell whether James M. Cox knew his contributions would establish a foundation for what is today known as Cox Communications – a Fortune 500 company with one of the highest-capacity and most reliable broadband delivery networks in the world.

COX COMMUNICATIONS'
MANCHESTER OFFICE AT
170 UTOPIA ROAD.

With a history tracing back to 1898, Cox Communications' entrepreneurial spirit and commitment to education is deeply rooted in Cox Enterprises Inc., shareholder of Cox Communications. Ohio schoolteacher turned governor, James M. Cox, is undoubtedly a cornerstone in the company's existence. His colorful and committed life even had him running for president of the United States in 1920. Though this proved unsuccessful, the purchase of his first newspaper, the Dayton Evening News, and his later acquisition of radio and television stations helped establish a company that would reach annual revenues of more than $8 billion. Throughout, Cox Communications' philosophy has remained strong: to be the recognized leader in the communications business, driven by quality and committed to its customers, employees and communities through innovation and growth.

As the nation's fourth-largest cable television provider, Cox Communications serves approximately 6.5 million customers, including 19 communities here in the state of Connecticut. In the 1970s, Meriden was the first in the state to receive services, and in 1997 the city was also the first system in New England to launch Cox's data and telephone services. Today, Cox provides an array of communications and entertainment services, such as high-speed Internet access under the Cox Business Internet brand. Cox's Transparent LAN data services, private line, Cox Digital Telephone and Business Centrex options are complemented with an array of video solutions via Cox Business Services, a Rhode Island-based division with major offices in nearby Manchester.

"With Cox Business Services there is never any 'one size fits all,'" says Mark Scott, vice president of Cox Business Services in New England, about the flexibility Cox has via its full-service network. Cox has invested more than $150 million in a hybrid-fiber coax network in Connecticut that provides customers with a true facilities-based communications alternative. The company helps businesses of all sizes become more efficient through the use of a full range of communications services to home offices, small, medium and large-sized businesses, schools and hospitality establishments, and government and military properties.

Cox Business Services' expertise is extensive, but truly unique in its approach. "We believe in partnering with the customer and tailoring the right combination of services to fit the need of each business," says Scott. He explains, "The local telephone company has its own lines, own poles and switching equipment. Typical competitive service providers are often dependent on the phone company for the use of their lines and sometimes switching equipment." Cox Communications, unlike so many others, delivers services such as local and long distance telephone, data transport solutions, wide area networks and virtual private networks over its own advanced hybrid-fiber coax broadband network. There is no middleman with Cox.

Companies might find that with resale service, their flexibility is hampered. Again, Cox has the upper hand because of its facilities-based status. "Our customers can get the whole gambit," says Scott. One of the strengths Cox Communications can offer is the bundling of several services from one company. Selecting Cox ensures that customers do not need to look any further for phone, Internet, long-distance or cable. Bundling these services together without eliminating the customers' options allows Cox to deliver its services in a more cost effective manner; this single platform has proven incredibly unique and valuable for the customer.

According to Scott, "Our local presence and participation in the community is an integral part of the Cox philosophy." Here in the New England area, Cox is responsible for contributing an estimated $5.2 million in both cash and in-kind resources each year supporting local charitable efforts focused on youth and education initiatives. Connecticut alone received approximately $2.1 million in charitable contributions. Cox's involvement in the community manifests itself in many ways, including its position as the national technology partner of the Boys & Girls Clubs. As part of this partnership, the Boys & Girls Club in Meriden receives courtesy cable and data services as well as grants to support the club's after school programming. Cox employees also donate their time, volunteering at the club and engaging in community service projects. Another exciting way that Cox involves itself in the community is through the Cable in the Classroom and Line to Learning programs. By supplying courtesy cable and high-speed data services to accredited schools within Connecticut service areas, the programs promote teaching and learning via broadband services.

Over the years, Cox has been extremely proud of the services it provides its customers, but it is also proud of its ability to actively contribute to the economy. It is estimated that Cox New England contributes $316 million to the Rhode Island and Connecticut economies and invests millions of dollars of private resources to bring new technologies and programs to its customers. With more than 350 employees in Connecticut, and with the increasing rate at which people and busi-

nesses are choosing Cox for their phone and Internet services, employment and customer growth will no doubt continue at a phenomenal rate.

Cox Business Services, as part of Cox Communications, is driven by several powerful advantages, including superior network and technology, a solid financial position and most importantly, a locally based customer service team of dedicated professionals. Because Cox owns and maintains its own network, it is directly responsible and accountable for customer service needs, something that Cox takes very seriously. "It is very important here at Cox Business Services that we provide customers a competitive choice, and that we are a company the customer can rely on and trust," says Scott. It seems that the goal at Cox Communications – to be the best company to work for and do business with in New England and nationally – is well within reach.

CONNECTICUT PUBLIC BROADCASTING INC.

Seeking to enrich people's lives through high-quality, educational programming has been the heart of what is known as Connecticut Public Broadcasting Inc. for more than 40 years.

CONNECTICUT PUBLIC BROADCASTING'S NEW BROADCAST HEADQUARTERS AT 1049 ASYLUM AVENUE IN HARTFORD.

*M*uch has changed over the years, but the mission of this organization has remained steadfast: Connecticut Public Broadcasting Inc. (CPBI) adds value to people's lives through programs and services that inform, educate, entertain and inspire audiences in Connecticut and beyond. CPBI, a nonprofit and noncommercial network, diligently focuses its program philosophy on making a difference for children, but also offers fair and balanced programming to the rest of its audiences.

CPBI's beginnings stretch back to 1962 in the basement of the Trinity College library, where a motivated and dedicated group began broadcasting from the Connecticut Educational Television station. For years, and on a minimal budget, they worked to enrich lives through high-quality programming, and the station eventually was renamed Connecticut Public Television (CPTV). In 1978, the network was joined by Connecticut Public Radio (WNPR), forming what is now known as Connecticut Public Broadcasting Inc.

Today, amidst a rebirth in downtown Hartford, CPBI embarks on an adventure of its own. On September 13, 2004, CPTV and WNPR left their location near Trinity College, and began settling in at their new location: 1049 Asylum Ave. in Hartford. The state-of-the-art facility sits on 2.75 acres of land, and with six stories and more than

62,000 square feet of space, CPBI can't help thinking it has come a long way since its days in the basement. Additionally, CPBI headquarters are attached to a 5,600-square-foot building housing two high-definition (HD) television studios, making CPTV the largest HD broadcast facility in the state. These milestones in CPBI's history have facilitated the continued growth and success of its programming. Today, with a $21 million budget, CPTV and WNPR reach an estimated 750,000 television viewers and over 221,000 radio listeners each week.

Without a doubt, CPTV remains most dedicated to its largest audience – children. A commitment to eleven and a half hours a day of noncommercial programming for children separates CPTV from other stations and makes it the only educational channel that genuinely has its viewers' best interests at heart. CPTV and its audiences were enriched with the creation of "Barney & Friends." To the creators and viewers, the show's success revealed that in a world dominated by "Sesame Street," there was indeed room for other children's shows.

The remainder of CPTV programming is designated to serve the under-served public. In determining who this is, CPBI is always asking a series of questions. Will the program make a difference? What kind of impact will it have? Will the program fill a need? The decision to broadcast the University of Connecticut women's basketball games is one such example. Although the community marketplace covered a few of the games, the remaining shows were not accessible to public viewers. Because University of Connecticut basketball has become such a phenomenon, CPBI has filled a great demand by broadcasting the games. In many ways, these games have become synonymous with CPBI. Often times, if the community marketplace is not covering events of importance like sports or public affairs, CPBI steps in. Also dedicated to relaying Connecticut stories through in-depth documentaries, CPBI is proud of its ability to work with independent producers.

On the radio front, WNPR, a National Public Radio affiliate, offers listeners the most popular programs on public radio today, including "Morning Edition," "All Things Considered," "Car Talk" and "A Prairie Home Companion." In addition, WNPR's Connecticut-based news team (often covering local issues with a national impact) and classical music format have earned the station accolades from around the state and nation. It has twice been honored with the coveted Peabody Award and has earned four consecutive Mark Twain Awards for Overall Station Excellence. Plus, "The Faith Middleton Show" continues to be a perennial favorite among listeners. The show spotlights great conversation with intriguing guests on a diverse array of topics and issues, weekdays on WNPR. In recognition of Faith's loyal listenership, she has been voted Best Local Radio Talk Show Host in Connecticut for seven years in a row.

Keeping up with broadcasting's ever changing and evolving technological innovations has been a significant part of CPBI's past and undoubtedly its future. Having gone from analog to digital, CPBI has seen the power of digital technology and is confident it has the power to revolutionize the broadcast industry in the 21st century. Digital technology not only improves television picture quality and radio sound quality, it also offers the power of connection. CPBI is planning to use digital technology to link a number of civic groups together to further enrich Connecticut's reservoir of educational, informational, civic and cultural resources. By linking government, higher education, libraries, museums, public health agencies, schools and civic groups, strong individual agencies become stronger, using one another as a resource. This five-year program is appropriately called Connecting

the Assets of Connecticut.

In conjunction with existing and new institutional partners, CPBI must determine how to best harness digital technology and its power to provide universal opportunity in Connecticut. Jerry Franklin, president and CEO of Connecticut Public Broadcasting Inc., hopes that as the digital world continues to unfold, the organization will continue to expand its services, including broadcasting from more than one signal. "We are very bullish on the future," Franklin says. "Our new facility is designed for us to take advantage of everything the new technology has to offer." And CPBI intends to do just that.

Working to evolve and continually provide quality programming comes with challenges. From its inception, funding has been one of CPBI's greatest challenges for two main reasons. In the very beginning, when licenses were made available to CPTV, there was no funding stream established and therefore, no money readily available. Secondly, because CPBI provides commercial-free broadcasting, traditional income from advertisers is nonexistent. CPBI has always been faced with generating revenue in alternative ways. Today, with no state funding and little federal funding (approximately $2 million of the annual budget is federally funded), CPBI relies heavily on fund raising to cover costs. There is no doubt that the enormous support received over the past 40 years from members, contributors to the Partners for a Digital Connecticut campaign, major donors, corporate underwriters and business partners, has made CPBI into what it is today. It is with much gratitude and appreciation that CPBI looks towards its own future and to meeting the future needs of those it serves.

THREE TELEVISION BROADCAST SERVICES ORIGINATE FROM CPBI'S NETWORK OPERATIONS CENTER (NOC) – CPTV, CPTV 2 AND A HIGH-DEFINITION (HDTV) PROGRAMMING STREAM FOR VIEWERS WHO HAVE HD TELEVISION SETS. THE NOC ALSO HOUSES WNPR'S RADIO BROADCAST EQUIPMENT AND A SOPHISTICATED TRANSMISSION SYSTEM THAT PROVIDES SATELLITE AND FIBER CONNECTIVITY TO TELEVISION FACILITIES THROUGHOUT THE U.S.

GREATER HARTFORD CONVENTION & VISITORS BUREAU

The Greater Hartford Convention & Visitors Bureau helps individuals and businesses of all sizes "Plan, Book and Play" in New England's Rising Star with the greatest of ease.

Charged with enhancing the economic fabric and quality of life in Hartford by marketing the city as a premier destination for national, regional and statewide conventions, the Greater Hartford Convention & Visitors Bureau (GHCVB) has been creating a buzz within the meeting planner market. The bottom line is that Hartford is getting noticed.

Thanks to the GHCVB's aggressive sales and marketing efforts, the meeting and convention industry is discovering that Hartford's "building boom" is providing convention-goers easy access to ample meeting space and lodging. As the Connecticut Convention Center joins the Hartford Civic Center and the Connecticut Expo Center, meeting and convention space in Hartford totals 740,000 square feet. Additionally, visitors may choose from more than 6,000 hotel rooms throughout Greater Hartford.

The Hartford region, marketed by the GHCVB, offers convention amenities of a

THE GREATER HARTFORD CONVENTION & VISITORS BUREAU TEAM, FROM LEFT: DEBORAH RYAN-PELLETIER, VICE PRESIDENT OF SALES; H. SCOTT PHELPS, PRESIDENT; CURT JENSEN, NATIONAL SALES MANAGER; SUE KOZCKA, NATIONAL SALES MANAGER; THERESA REYNOLDS, DIRECTOR OF MEMBERSHIP; GINA LYNCH, SALES AND MARKETING MANAGER; PHYLLIS ANDERSON, NATIONAL SALES MANAGER AND KAREN STAPLES, NATIONAL SALES MANAGER.

much larger metropolis without the hassle and big city price. The sales team keeps Hartford visible by attending national and regional trade shows, sponsoring events, hosting telemarketing blitzes and familiarization tours, responding to leads and RFPs, and through targeted sales missions.

Hartford continues to attract groups into the city for national or regional conferences through the Bring it Home to Hartford program. It's easy to participate; companies

are able to contact industry colleagues and association members to promote Hartford as a meeting destination. GHCVB sales staff follows up with marketing materials, site familiarization tours and proposals and then, once Hartford has been chosen as the host city, event coordination services.

The GHCVB collaborates with meeting planners to make events a success by providing assistance including: coordination with hotels to establish room blocks and proposals; supply of visitors' guides, maps and other promotional materials; coordination of site inspections; on-site logistics and registration assistance; promotion for the event to group members and media; and planing of pre- and post-conference activities.

In 2003, the GHCVB won *Facilities & Destinations Magazine*'s Top Destination Award for the fifth consecutive year. In 2004, the GHCVB received the Pinnacle Award from *Successful Meetings* magazine for the fourth time in five years. Both awards represent excellence among destination marketing organizations in the meetings industry.

The GHCVB, which celebrated its 30th anniversary in 2004, is a public-private partnership working with Hartford's businesses, institutions, nonprofits and surrounding communities to market the region as a meeting destination. GHCVB works closely with the Capital City Economic Development Authority, the Connecticut Convention Center and the Greater Hartford region's hospitality community and state tourism organizations.

GHCVB's members, which consist of more than 200 corporations, educational, cultural and arts institutions, hospitals and health care organizations, meeting and lodging facilities, and restaurants, benefit from the variety of referrals, networking, marketing and meeting coordination services that are available. The GHCVB is the liaison in the middle of a win-win relationship, connecting newcomers to Hartford with the arts, culture, entertainment and history that Hartford has to offer.

GRUNBERG REALTY

Grunberg Realty **hopes to build on the success it has enjoyed in Manhattan by establishing a strong presence in the re-emerging city of Hartford.**

G runberg Realty prides itself on excellent service and a feeling of community at each of its properties. The firm's mission is to offer its tenants exceptional amenities, quality and service so its buildings' occupants can concentrate on making their businesses grow instead of dealing with standard of living issues. World-class appearance and service, coupled with affordability, is what tenants can expect in a Grunberg-owned and managed property.

The company established itself in Hartford in 2003 with the purchase of the Medical Arts Building at 21 Woodland St. and most recently closed on 280 Trumbull St., one of the city's premier office towers in the Central Business District. The company is pleased with the quality and pace of improvements being made throughout the city and plans to add to those improvements by developing its own properties in parallel ways. One of numerous improvements being made to 280 Trumbull St. is a renovation of the lobby. A waiting area has been introduced, complete with an antique Persian rug, tapestries, comfortable leather chairs, sofas and a piano playing over the sound of falling water from a 19-foot high wall of water.

In addition to the Trumbull Street renovations, the Medical Arts Building is also being refurbished inside and out. From roof to parking lot, from chillers to boilers, and from handicapped-accessible entrance doors to state-of-the-art security and lighting, Grunberg Realty is focused on tenant satisfaction and the reduction of long-term operating expenses.

Grunberg Realty is committed to Hartford. The firm plans to make 280 Trumbull St. its showcase property in the city and hopes to increase its presence as the area grows and flourishes. The company is proud that it is expanding and that it is able to continue moving into new markets like Hartford. Hiring local talent to manage and staff its buildings is a practice that distinguishes the company from its competitors. Hartford natives serve Hartford tenants by customizing their services to fit the particular needs of their market and occupants.

Grunberg Realty is proud to have a tenant list that reads like a Who's Who of the business community. It has included Prudential Financial, Robinson & Cole LLP, CIGNA, Chase Enterprises, UPS Capital, O'Connell, Flaherty & Attmore, The Hutensky Group, IKON Office Solutions, Cushman & Wakefield, Levin, Ford & Paulekas LLP, Annuity & Life RE, Hudson United Bank, Kern & Wooley, NLRB, Colin Services, CT Corporation System, Corporation for National Service & Community, and Total Communications.

Grunberg Realty has bought, managed and repositioned commercial and residential properties for more than 40 years. Zvi and Fanny Grunberg, its founders, came to New York in 1962 and worked tirelessly managing their own residential properties. In 1989, Zvi passed away, leaving Fanny as chief executive officer though Zvi's influence continues on in his sons, Michael and Ariel.

Since the turn of the new century, the company has focused on purchasing commercial properties and believes that Hartford has many desirable opportunities still available. Grunberg Realty hopes to play an important role in Hartford's future success.

PART OF THE WEST FAÇADE OF 280 TRUMBULL ST. AS SEEN FROM THE CORNER OF TRUMBULL AND CHURCH STREETS.

GREATER HARTFORD ARTS COUNCIL

Now the 10th largest United Arts fund in the country, and the largest independent arts council in New England, the Greater Hartford Arts Council provides grants and services to more than 100 local arts and heritage organizations each year.

PHOTO/STUART FELDMAN

THE GREATER HARTFORD ARTS COUNCIL FUNDS AND PRODUCES FAVORITE COMMUNITY EVENTS THAT DRAW HUNDREDS OF THOUSANDS OF PEOPLE TO DOWNTOWN HARTFORD EACH YEAR.

From its creation in 1971 to support five core arts groups, the Greater Hartford Arts Council certainly has grown. It also has earned a national reputation as a leader in diversified services and cultural promotions. Each year, the Arts Council's United Arts campaign raises money from individuals, corporations, foundations and public sources to fund a wide spectrum of grant programs. Over the years, it has invested more than $38 million dollars in the region's arts and heritage community. That investment has paid off. The region's cultural assets greatly enhance the area's quality of life, and make it a more attractive destination for families and businesses. In fact, Places Rated Almanac ranks Greater Hartford in the top six percent of all metro areas in North America for arts and culture.

In addition to providing a stable source of operating support to nearly three dozen arts and heritage groups each year, the Greater Hartford Arts Council also funds special programming for children, families and neighborhoods. Events and public art projects in the city of Hartford are also funded, along with fellowships to individual artists.

To help residents and visitors enjoy the tremendous programming these groups have to offer, the Greater Hartford Arts Council offers an online searchable cultural calendar at *www.ConnectTheDots.org*. Its 7-Day Arts & Entertainment Forecast weekly e-mail keeps tens of thousands of readers up-to-date on what's happening in Hartford. Its "Let's GO!" membership program offers money-saving deals on entertainment, dining and more to arts supporters. And, the Greater Hartford Arts Council is a founding member of the Hartford Image Project, which promotes the city through the "Hartford, New England's Rising Star" campaign.

Helping children to learn about the arts is another Arts Council priority. It works with schools to bring visiting artists to classrooms, and offers a teen arts apprenticeship program that helps young people master both art and career skills.

This is not your average arts council. You won't find another in the country that picks up trash, but the Greater Hartford Arts Council does through its Hartford Proud & Beautiful affiliate – more than 100 tons of litter per year, in fact. It also beautifies the city by cleaning graffiti and adding colorful flowerpots and lively banners to city streets. And if you stop in the Greater Hartford Welcome Center at 45 Pratt St. to pick up a brochure or get advice on a good restaurant, you'll be talking to an Arts Council staff member.

Producing community events is another Arts Council strong suit. Each year, it produces such community favorites as the Hartford Festival of Light®, Connecticut Veterans Day Parade and even the victory parades for the UConn basketball teams.

Finding innovative and artistic ways to enliven and enrich Connecticut's Capital Region has been a Greater Hartford Arts Council specialty for more than 30 years, and it will continue to brighten our community's future for years to come.

LUIS OF HARTFORD

The success of home furnishings retailer Luis of Hartford not only represents Carlos Lopez's savvy business skills, it also represents his dedication to the city of Hartford and his commitment to make Park Street into a lively, desirable destination spot.

CARLOS LOPEZ, IN HIS FURNITURE SHOWROOM LOCATED ON PARK STREET.

Luis of Hartford has been selling quality home furnishings at 709 Park St. since 1972. In 1976, Carlos Lopez, a native Cuban, decided to buy the business from Luis Hernandez, with whom he had been working to develop a strong brand name and a dedicated clientele. The store has grown significantly in size and revenue since its humble beginnings, but it still offers a high-quality, eclectic assortment of home furnishings at competitive prices to many of the same families it served in the '70s.

Lopez is proud of the success of Luis of Hartford, which still continues to be family-managed and operated. He employs nine people, four of whom have worked at the store for more than 15 years. Carlos Lopez prides himself on being a fair manager and never takes for granted the people around him.

Despite the store's continued success, Lopez is humble about his achievements. He is committed to providing a valuable service as owner of Luis of Hartford, but values his involvement in the community above everything else. He has owned the block of Park Street where Luis of Hartford is located for more than 25 years and has donated space for a police substation since 1994. In 1990, in conjunction with Broad Park Development, he developed El Mercado, a nationally recognized Latin style, eight-store shopping center that includes a grocery store, travel agency, restaurants, jewelry retailer and wire service. Lopez increased occupancy from 45 percent to 100 percent in a very short period of time and maintains that occupancy rate today.

Lopez works with the Spanish American Merchants' Association (SAMA) and the Park Street Special Service District to make Park Street a more recognized destination spot for people of all ethnic backgrounds looking to experience the Latino culture. One of SAMA's undertakings is the oversight of a $7 million "streetscape" project to rebuild Park Street. New brick sidewalks, light posts, trees, traffic lights and covered bus stops are just a few of the improvements being made.

To maintain the street once it is rebuilt, Lopez, along with eight other board members of the Park Street Special Service District, is working to improve three main areas: safety, parking and cleanliness. The group has raised money, by donations, grants and self-imposed taxes, to fund a "street ambassador" to maintain safety and provide services for visitors such as recharging dead car batteries, unlocking cars and tending to small medical emergencies. Money is also being raised to hire maintenance staff and parking lot attendants.

Carlos Lopez hopes that one day in the not-so-distant future, the block that houses the largest Hispanic furniture store in New England will also be a destination spot for the Hispanic community, similar to cities in Florida and Texas. By making the neighborhood a more supportive place for merchants and shoppers, Lopez, along with SAMA and other community groups, is working to change the negative perception that has plagued it in the past. As the man responsible for more than doubling occupancy rates of El Mercado, and with past and current involvement with groups such as the United Way of the Capital Area, the Connecticut Economic Development Fund and Hartford Hospital, Carlos Lopez is confident that he can make a difference towards accomplishing that goal.

The future looks brighter for the Greater Hartford area thanks to businesses like Connecticut Lighting Centers, a vibrant, dynamic company that has been providing state-of-the-art lighting and lighting solutions for more than 30 years.

Connecticut Lighting Centers' Hartford showroom is located at 160 Brainard Road, off exit 27 on I-91.

David Director, president of this family-owned business, considers the company's history – its small beginnings and strong and steady growth – with every decision that he makes. It is a consideration that David finds critical not only to the fiscal health of the corporation, but to the company's prominent reputation in the lighting industry, among customers and among the business community in Greater Hartford.

Connecticut Lighting Centers' Hartford location was first introduced to Arthur Director, David's father, in 1972. At that time, the lighting center concept was fairly new and the Hartford retail store was not doing well; it was on the verge of bankruptcy. One of the company's principals, who happens to be David's godfather, sought Arthur's help. Arthur was known as an astute businessman who was employed as an executive with the Red Wing Oil Company, a large regional distributor of gasoline, heating oils and heating equipment that had just been acquired by a major oil company. Arthur was unhappy with his current position and was quite eager to consider a new employment opportunity with this new business venture.

He took a two-week vacation from Red Wing Oil, observed and evaluated the situation at Connecticut Lighting, and with a handshake, became a partner in the corpo-

ration, assuming his share of the $250,000 business debt. Arthur was quite confident that under the right management, significant potential for the retail business could be realized. Soon enough, the whole family lived the business, including his wife Edythe, who served as a buyer of lamps and lighting accessories.

Twenty-two years later, in 1994, David assumed the company presidency when Arthur retired. David, a cum laude graduate of Quinnipiac University, enjoys the constantly changing world of business and loves the lighting business. He says, "I love what I do. The business is dynamic and changing every day. The challenge is always there."

The family values taught in the Director home were naturally invoked in the workplace.

Despite significant changes in the general business environment over the years, throughout all of the stages of the company's dramatic growth, the basic principles and policies established by the Director family remain steadfast and as strong as ever.

One of the most important values is giving back to the community that supports you. With a family of his own and the family business to run, David works hard to give back to the community. Both Arthur and David are extremely proud of the time, energy and support they have given throughout the years to such organizations as the Rushford Center, United Way,

Middletown Rotary Club, Connecticut Association of Schools, Interfaith Golf Tournament, B'nai Brith, Northern Middlesex YMCA, Nutmeg Big Brothers Big Sisters and the Better Business Bureau of Connecticut. Many other agencies in the Greater Hartford area have benefited in the past, and continue to do so today, from the generosity of Connecticut Lighting Centers. The Directors strongly believe that their business success is directly linked to their involvement in their community.

Connecticut Lighting Centers lives its motto, "We sell solutions, not lighting." With more than 70 employees, a number of whom have been with the company for more than 25 years, the staff at Connecticut Lighting Centers is extremely knowledgeable about the products they sell. They are well trained to meet the requirements of demanding customers and are eager to

assist with any and all lighting and decorating needs.

David and his staff pride themselves on providing a full-service lighting experience. The presentation in the lighting showrooms is extraordinary; walls, ceilings, tabletops and floors beautifully display the vast selection of merchandise available – the largest collection of lighting, ceiling fans and home accents in all of New England. David and his sales team are convinced that if you can't find what you are looking for at Connecticut

Lighting, you may not find it anywhere!

Over the years, the company has grown and matured, providing both residential and commercial lighting as well as design services. Despite the state-of-the-art solutions that the Connecticut Lighting Centers provide, the Director family remains 'old-fashioned' in the way that they run the business. The strength of the drive to make the customer happy has remained constant since Arthur entered into the lighting business. A plaque with a poem sits prominently on David's desk. His father gave it to him when he first entered into the business. It's called, "Who's the Boss?" The poem eloquently states the Director family business fundamental: "There's only one boss, and whether a person shines shoes for a living or heads up the largest corporation in the world, the boss remains the same. It's the customer!"

The Director family and the Connecticut Lighting Centers' staff have made every effort to embrace their community, and their community has certainly embraced them back. Customers quickly become friends and spread the word. The extraordinary rate of repeat business and new customer growth has enabled Connecticut Lighting Centers to provide quality, selection and service like no other provider of lighting and lighting solutions in the Greater Hartford area, and to remain consistently generous in its support of the Greater Hartford community.

ARTHUR DIRECTOR AND SON DAVID DIRECTOR HAVE BOTH BEEN HONORED BY THE MIDDLESEX CHAMBER OF COMMERCE AS "CITIZEN OF THE YEAR" – ONLY THE SECOND FATHER/SON TEAM TO RECEIVE THE HONOR.

HOME ACCENTS OF ALL TYPES ARE SHOWN THROUGHOUT BOTH STORES.

HUGHES & CRONIN — PUBLIC AFFAIRS STRATEGIES INC.

Since 1974, Hughes & Cronin has maintained its position as one of the top 10 lobbying firms in Connecticut*, a fact in which the company takes great pride, considering the incredible recent industry growth.

FROM LEFT, LOBBYISTS CARROLL J. HUGHES AND JEAN CRONIN POSITION THEMSELVES IN THE FAMILIAR HALLWAYS OF THE STATE CAPITOL.

PHOTO/STEVE LASCHEVER

In 1974, Hughes & Cronin, the first independently established lobbying firm in Connecticut, was the only lobbying firm.

Today, with more than 30 firms competing in the state, Hughes & Cronin has maintained a legacy and reputation like no other to provide the most fundamental and comprehensive lobbying services.

After working in local and state government for many years, Carroll J. Hughes, with only three accounts, left and went into business for himself. Years of experience and a unique understanding of the political process allowed Hughes to provide the best representation for corporate clients, associations and nonprofit organizations. Now with seven employees, including his wife, Jean Cronin, and his son, Joshua Hughes, business has grown significantly. Throughout this growth, Hughes & Cronin has been consistently selected to represent national, regional and state groups in Connecticut, specifically because of the solid record and standard of service for which the company is known.

Hughes & Cronin, a full-service government relations, public affairs and association management firm, provides an array of services including: legislative lobbying in Hartford; state agency administrative lobbying; full-service association management, communications and function management; media relations; as well as municipal relations, legal services and lobbying. The relatively small staff of lobbyists has a combined force of more than 80 years of state and local government experience in Connecticut.

In the company's 30 years of business, it has worked tirelessly to learn every detail of its clients' issues so it can strategize accordingly. For lobbyists, the test is to be able to keep up to speed with queries and concerns of agency and legislative staff on a particular issue. This is a daunting task that the experienced and knowledgeable professionals at Hughes & Cronin take very seriously. In-depth, on-site reviews and evaluations conducted with clients allow the staff to effectively present the issues to legislators and government officials at all levels. Constant monitoring and analyzing of proposals and ideas early on allows the company to assist clients' efforts in shaping the issues rather than reacting to them later. Additionally, the use of long-term media contacts and other sources provides an information network that helps Hughes & Cronin identify issues early in the process.

The hard work and dedication provided by Hughes & Cronin is the reason it remains one of the top 10 lobbying firms in Connecticut. The quality of accounts retained by the company and the staff's years of representation is a reflection of the superior and personal service the company provides.

In the ever-changing relationship between business and government, the laws passed at the State Capitol may impact your business. For this reason, the knowledgeable and professional staff at Hughes & Cronin — Public Affairs Strategies, Inc. remains as important as ever in intimately representing the diverse interests of Hartford's business community.

* Based on information from the State of Connecticut Ethics Commission.

MADISON SQUARE GARDEN — CONNECTICUT

Madison Square Garden – Connecticut **began** managing the Hartford Civic Center in 1997 through an agreement with the Connecticut Development Authority and has entertained millions of visitors annually since then.

PHOTOS/JERRY MARGOLIS

TOP LEFT –
HARTFORD WOLF PACK HOCKEY

TOP RIGHT – UCONN MEN'S
BASKETBALL AT THE CIVIC CENTER

BOTTOM LEFT – UCONN FOOTBALL
GAME AT RENTSCHLER FIELD

BOTTOM RIGHT – BRUCE
SPRINGSTEEN & THE E STREET
BAND LIVE AT RENTSCHLER FIELD

Madison Square Garden – Connecticut is the facility manager for both the Hartford Civic Center Veterans Memorial Coliseum and Exhibition Center and East Hartford's Rentschler Field, lending its extensive expertise in event and facility operations to these two premier sports and entertainment venues in the state of Connecticut. The combination of the Civic Center and Rentschler Field caters to a wide variety of local, national and international sporting and entertainment events, as well as trade shows, meetings and conferences.

The Hartford Civic Center Veterans Memorial Coliseum has been Connecticut's premier indoor sports and entertainment facility since 1975. It entertains millions of guests annually with a variety of concerts, family shows, ice-skating spectaculars, consumer events and trade shows throughout each season. Concert headliners include the Rolling Stones, Elton John, Billy Joel, Bon Jovi, U2, Andrea Bocelli, Britney Spears, Pavarotti and Paul McCartney. Annual attractions include Ringling Bros. and Barnum & Bailey, Sesame Street Live, World Wrestling Entertainment, Stars on Ice, Champions on Ice, the CMTA Boat Show, the Hartford Bridal Expo and the Original Connecticut Home Show. Special Events have included the NHL Entry Draft and All Star Game, World Figure Skating Championships, NBA and WNBA basketball games, Championship Boxing, NCAA Tournaments, WWE's WrestleMania XI, and the Disney Annual Shareholders Meeting. In addition to the high-profile events held throughout the year, the Civic Center also serves as the home of the Hartford Wolf Pack (AHL affiliate of the New York Rangers) and is the proud host of the Big East Conference Women's Basketball Championship. It is also the home away from home for the University of Connecticut men's and women's basketball programs.

In 2003, Madison Square Garden – CT began managing Rentschler Field. As Connecticut's new sports and entertainment stadium, the brand new 40,000-seat facility was developed by the state of Connecticut's Office of Policy and Management, and is named for Pratt & Whitney aircraft founder Frederick Rentschler. The stadium, which is built on a former airfield donated by Pratt & Whitney, is the new home of the University of Connecticut Huskies football team, and hosts various athletic competitions, entertainment and civic events, special events, conferences, banquets, and corporate functions. In its inaugural season the stadium hosted nine major events, including six UConn football games, the opening ceremonies of the State Games of America and two Bruce Springsteen concerts. Approximately 300,000 spectators attended these events. During the football off-season, Rentschler has played host to various national, international and local events such as soccer, rugby and high school football.

Madison Square Garden is continually showing its commitment not only to the facilities it manages, but to the Greater Hartford community and the state of Connecticut as well.

It looks forward to welcoming guests to events at the Hartford Civic Center Veterans Memorial Coliseum and Exhibition Center, as well as the new Rentschler Field.

Steve Giarratana/QualityPhotograph.com

1978—2002

HORTON INTERNATIONAL LLC

Horton International LLC is committed to serving Connecticut's executive recruiting needs. The firm offers a consultative approach, objectivity and value as key elements of its retained search practice.

PHOTO/STEVE LASCHEVER

MEMBERS OF THE HORTON INTERNATIONAL TEAM IN THEIR WEST HARTFORD OFFICE.

*H*orton International LLC is an international executive search firm serving a broad base of clients in Connecticut, the United States and across the globe. Partners Larry Brown and Bob Gilchrist manage the U.S. search business from their headquarters in West Hartford, Connecticut, and coordinate cross-border and international search assignments with their partners in Horton International's 29 other offices in Europe, Latin America and Asia. Members of the Horton International team bring a broad range of industry experience and a high level of professionalism to the search process and build strong and enduring partnerships with their clients.

Horton International serves a broad cross-selection of industries and recruits board level and executive talent in all functional areas, including general management, finance, human resources, marketing, manufacturing and engineering. Its clients include start-up businesses and mid-market firms, as well as Fortune 100 companies. Although Horton International is large enough to provide the necessary resources and expertise to meet global recruiting needs, it provides the intimacy of a small firm with a commitment to quality, personal attention and lasting relationships.

That relationship is built around Horton International's commitment to balancing its dual responsibilities of providing clients with outstanding talent, practical solutions and professional advice, while at the same time providing candidates with an honest representation of an opportunity with a client. Horton International's reliance on search professionals with industry savvy and prior successful business careers provides its clients with an advantage; their organizational needs are understood quickly and accurately.

Besides building a strong relationship with both clients and candidates, Horton International undertakes extensive research and provides its clients access to the very best talent. As a retained executive search firm, Horton International provides objective advice on all candidates, internal and external, as its fee is not contingent on the hiring of one specific individual. Finally, Horton International emphasizes value by providing only the most qualified candidates along with accurate and comprehensive assessments of their experience and organizational "fit."

Horton International LLC maintains a strong commitment to Connecticut's businesses and industries while continuing to expand its U.S. and Americas presence.

HARTFORD DENTAL GROUP

From the staff's genuine, caring and attentive response to patient phone calls, to the friendly smiles greeting patients upon arrival, the Hartford Dental Group is not your typical dentist's office.

THE RECEPTION AREA AT THE HARTFORD DENTAL GROUP'S OFFICE IS DESIGNED TO RELAX EVEN THE MOST APPREHENSIVE PATIENT — COMPLETE WITH AUTHENTIC THEATER-STYLE SEATING, DIMMED LIGHTS AND A MOVIE SCREEN.

The University of Connecticut School of Dental Medicine brought the late Dr. Norman Mendlinger to Connecticut and eventually to Hartford. Dr. Mendlinger, the founder of the Hartford Dental Group, was one of the original instructors at the university when its first students graduated in 1972. Dr. Mendlinger enjoyed the collaborative environment of the dental school. Unlike the typical single-practitioner dental offices of the day, the dental school's professors worked together to educate the students and provide all phases of dental treatment. Inspired by the dental school to provide the most broad-based dental care available, Dr. Mendlinger established one of Connecticut's first private group dental practices, the Hartford Dental Group.

The Hartford Dental Group opened in 1980 at 21 Woodland St., between Asylum and Farmington avenues – an active, pedestrian-friendly area. With Saint Francis Hospital and Medical Center, several insurance companies, and the University of Connecticut School of Law within walking distance, the Hartford Dental Group quickly built a base of loyal patients. With appointments in high demand, the Hartford Dental Group soon added general dentists, specialists and hygienists to its staff.

Growth continued, and the Hartford Dental Group expanded to its current state-of-the-art facility with a staff of 10 dentists and three hygienists. True to its mission to offer broad-based dental care, the Hartford Dental Group not only provides its patients with general dentistry, but also offers oral surgery, periodontal therapy, cosmetic and reconstructive dentistry including implants, teeth whitening, bonding and veneers; this is a true multi-specialty practice. The office provides early morning and late evening appointments in addition to Saturday appointments to accommodate its diverse patient population. Two decades after the Hartford Dental Group was founded, the practice maintains its commitment to its Asylum Hill and West End neighbors.

It takes just a moment to recognize that an appointment with Hartford Dental Group will be like no other. From the staff's genuine, caring and attentive response to patient phone calls, to the friendly smiles greeting patients upon arrival, the Hartford Dental Group is not your typical dentist's office. The patient lounge replicates a movie theater – complete with authentic theater-style seating, dimmed lights and a movie screen, all designed to relax even the most apprehensive patient.

The entire staff, from the clinical staff managed by Senior Dentist Dr. Ron Arbuckle to the administrative staff managed by Wendy Mendlinger, is committed to raising each patient's "Dental IQ." The Hartford Dental Group provides online, high-tech Web-based patient education, and more importantly, highlights the need for a patient's comprehension of any recommended treatment.

Dentistry and technology have changed, but Hartford Dental Group's mission remains the same: Providing optimal dental treatment to its current patients and welcoming new patients. As quoted by Senior Dentist Dr. Ron Arbuckle, "It is the people providing the dental care that make the difference. Hartford Dental Group's greatest asset is the quality and concern of its caring staff."

FREIGHTLINER OF HARTFORD INC.

The Freightliner Group **is the leading North American truck and specialty vehicle manufacturer, and is a major part of the world's largest and most influential commercial vehicle manufacturer – DaimlerChrysler. The firm is committed to maintaining a standard of technological innovation and excellence in quality.**

PHOTO/STEVE LASCHEVER

INDOOR SHOWROOM AT SALES FACILITY SHOWING, FROM LEFT, A FREIGHTLINER CORNADO AND COLUMBIA TRACTORS.

Longtime colleagues and friends Lindy Bigliazzi and Kenneth Wilson had worked together in the freight equipment business for nearly two decades, when in 1996, the pair approached the owner of an existing dealership in East Hartford about the possibility of selling the business. The timing of their inquiry was right and soon they were the new owners of Freightliner of Hartford.

Bigliazzi and Wilson launched their new venture with 18 employees. In an industry known for business conducted by instinct and a handshake, the duo's reputation earned them a solid start. Wherever Bigliazzi and Wilson went, customers followed. With just a single building on the five-acre property, and no showroom, Freightliner of Hartford's pledge that no customer would leave unsatisfied was the key to growth.

By 1998, the group was stretching the limits of its offices and services bays, and

more than 8,000 square feet of space was added to the main building. A year later, they purchased an existing 6,000-square-foot building with six service bays on an adjacent acre of land. Finally in 2000, Freightliner of Hartford's largest building was added to the property – a modern 18,000-square-foot sales showroom with office space for Freightliner staff. The dealership now has the capacity to service some 30 vehicles at a time and a customer-friendly showroom to display the latest Freightliner vehicles.

As Freightliner Group added brands to its product line, Freightliner of Hartford followed. Passers-by on Interstate 84 have a bird's eye view of Freightliner's ever-changing inventory, housed on their 11-acre campus. Freightliner of Hartford sells and services Freightliner heavy-duty highway tractors and medium-duty trucks, heavy vocational trucks and extreme-duty vehicles, Sprinter passenger and cargo vans and cabs, and American LaFrance fire and emergency rescue trucks. It also services Western Star premium sleeper tractors.

In less than a decade, Freightliner of Hartford tripled its sales and increased its employee roster from 18 to 90, many of whom have been with the company since its inception. They have ensured their success by catering not only to corporate accounts, but also to owner operators. Freightliner vehicles can be found transporting everything from dry goods to rubbish. Freightliner of Hartford sells and services vehicles for nearly every industry sector, including beverage, municipal, trash, dry-van, and does it with an assortment of trucks, including oil trucks, flat beds, dump trucks, and roll offs.

Freightliner of Hartford's customers are cared for by dedicated, honest, professional employees. Service technicians are certified by the National Institute for Automotive Service Excellence, the gold standard in professional automotive designations. More than 20 repair bays operate for at least 16 hours every day, accommodating the around-the-clock nature of the transportation industry.

Service personnel are supported by a parts department that stocks tens of thousands of items in its inventory – both Freightliner original equipment parts, as well as parts for competitive trucks. Maintenance customers have access to aftermarket parts from more than 150 vendors, including industry giants ArvinMeritor, Eaton, Caterpillar, Cummins and Detroit Diesel Corp. In the rare circumstance when a part is not on hand, Freightliner of Hartford can procure any item in 24 hours or less.

Freightliner of Hartford maintains corporate fleets for some 60 companies in Connecticut, and for national transportation companies such as Schneider National, J.B. Hunt and Penske Truck Leasing.

More than 50 municipalities in Connecticut bring their fire and rescue vehicles to Freightliner of Hartford, trusting the company to keep hundreds of thousands of dollars in equipment operating at peak performance. You may even see a Freightliner of Hartford sales representative driving an American LaFrance fire truck to municipalities across New England so fire safety professionals can examine the equipment on their home turf.

The very employees who contributed to Freightliner of Hartford's growth also helped save the company when it faced a fiscal crisis in 2001 and 2002. A sharp economic downturn, in which a vast majority of owner operators went out of business, brought an unexpected decline in revenue to the company that had just recently invested $3 million in its new showroom.

Lindy Bigliazzi and Kenneth Wilson were unwavering in their commitment to spare every employee the hardship of unemploy-

PHOTO/STEVE LASCHEVER

ment. Together with their workers, they evaluated every expenditure and process. Belts were tightened, and in spite of a near catastrophic loss of customers, not a single job was lost. Freightliner of Hartford retains that staff today, and has increased employment numbers by another 10 percent.

Freightliner of Hartford is one of the largest Freightliner dealers in New England and the fifth largest seller of American LaFrance in the country. While Freightliner of Hartford has grown, Bigliazzi and Wilson's dedication to their employees and customers has not gone unnoticed. They have earned loyalty and respect from their families, staff and transportation professionals who are in it with them for the long haul.

AN EXTERIOR VIEW OF THE EAST HARTFORD SERVICE FACILITY. FROM LEFT, COLUMBIA, SPRINTER AND CORNADO TRACTORS.

CONNECTICARE INC.

Known as "the company with a heart," ConnectiCare is dedicated to providing community service and offering affordable health plan options for small business owners.

CONNECTICARE'S CUSTOMER SERVICE REPRESENTATIVES ARE AMONG THE MOST RESPONSIVE IN THE INDUSTRY — ANSWERING MEMBER PHONE CALLS IN 12 SECONDS OR LESS.

Ranked as one of the fastest-growing HMOs in the state*, ConnectiCare prides itself on being a homegrown, locally run health plan where disease management is part of its core business.

Known as "the company with a heart," ConnectiCare is dedicated to providing community service and offering affordable health plan options for small business owners.

ConnectiCare has challenged the HMO Goliaths for marketshare in the Greater Hartford region for nearly 23 years and it has done so with remarkable success.

The relatively small, young health plan is ranked a solid third in size in the Nutmeg State, and has earned the loyalty and respect of the Greater Hartford business community. ConnectiCare says that its steady growth is a result of its local, accessible and customer-focused nature – all of which have established it as a premium brand.

Founded by a group of doctors from Hartford Hospital, ConnectiCare was born with the mission of establishing a health plan that would truly care about its members. Twenty-three years later and 550 employees strong, ConnectiCare still lives by that same mission, serving more than 270,000 individuals in Connecticut and Western Massachusetts today.

"We've built this company from the ground up with a culture where our customer is king," says Marcel "Gus" Gamache, president and CEO of ConnectiCare. "That's why we exist. We're here to make sure that our members get personalized service and access to the highest-quality medical care available without the hassle."

The company touts a high employee retention rate, noting that 12,000 people applied for the mere 20 open positions that became available last year. The company's employees, Gamache says, are critical to ConnectiCare's continuing success.

"Every employee owns the culture here at ConnectiCare," Gamache says. "They believe in it. They perpetuate it."

ConnectiCare has also been named an "Employer of Choice" in the Greater Hartford region, and was honored with the 2002 University of Hartford Business Leadership Award.

ConnectiCare has set its sights on becoming a regional carrier for years and has steadily been expanding beyond state lines. With its market expansion into Western Massachusetts, ConnectiCare's reach now extends up the Route 91 corridor all the way to the Vermont border. ConnectiCare is also stretching southeast into four counties in New York state to accommodate employer groups that are based in eastern Connecticut with employees living across New York state lines.

ConnectiCare recently announced that it has plans to be acquired by the Health Insurance Plan of Greater New York (HIP) to further strengthen its ability to grow.

"Our future viability is tied to our ability to respond to market needs quickly, by growing and launching new initiatives that keep health care affordable," Gamache says.

Although the company is excited about expansion opportunities, Gamache says that ConnectiCare has seen what has happened to other companies that have grown too fast. "We value our longstanding customers and won't do anything that would compromise our hallmark reputation for quality and service."

Based on information from the Connecticut Department of Insurance.

**Some of this content was paraphrased from an article that appeared in the Jan. 12, 2004, issue of the Hartford Business Journal.*

STOCKTON ASSOCIATES

For the last 23 years, Ed Stockton's passion for Connecticut has taken the form of Stockton Associates, which specializes in the use of economic analysis for the solution of real estate problems and opportunities.

PHOTO/IRA NOZIK

MARILYN AND ED STOCKTON AT THEIR BLOOMFIELD OFFICE.

As commissioner of economic development for Connecticut for six and a half years, Ed Stockton made a career out of promoting the state as a great place to live and work. Though no longer the commissioner, Stockton has never stopped believing that "there is no place like Connecticut." With a team of individuals with diverse capabilities, including his wife and business partner, Marilyn Stockton, Stockton Associates utilizes "unique capabilities rooted in economic expertise and international experience" to assist a variety of clients.

Ed Stockton's knowledge, understanding and experience with local, state and federal government, combined with Marilyn's background in real estate, education and graphic arts, serve as a remarkable resource for clients. The Stockton's shared love of traveling, coupled with their devotion to the state of Connecticut, has helped to establish Stockton Associates' niche in the international market. This consulting firm has corporate investor contacts throughout the world, and specializes in finding development opportunities for overseas companies in the United States. "Connecticut is extremely attractive to overseas companies," says Ed. "The state is known for being a leader in advanced technology and possesses a highly skilled work force from which these companies can draw." Those who do come to Connecticut are attracted to its "sophisticated popula-

tion." Connecticut, according to Stockton, really is a "unique and vibrant" place to live and work and international clients are excited for the opportunity to partake in this environment.

E/CONNomics, an economic consulting firm specializing in the analysis of the Connecticut economy, is also closely linked to Stockton Associates. Equipped with an extensive database, the company is capable of covering all aspects of statewide economic activity. With detailed information on labor force, personal income, wage rates, local taxes and more, the company can assist others in successful stratagems to "maximize opportunities and minimize problems." This information has proved priceless to companies within the region and abroad.

Over the years Ed Stockton has been applauded for his efforts in both government and trade. Most recently he was awarded the Todd Ouida World Trade Award for exemplifying the Connecticut World Trade Association's "objective of peace and stability through trade." Despite the accolades Ed has received over the years, he remains most proud of bringing in and creating more jobs for the citizens of Connecticut. Assisting international companies – such as Lego, Trumpf and Konica – set up in the state, as well as helping companies within the state find an international market in which to export their product, gives the Stocktons and those they work with a sense of a job well done.

HILB ROGAL & HOBBS

Hilb Rogal & Hobbs (HRH)

serves corporate and

private clients, assisting

them with their risk

management and insurance

programs, employee

benefits and financial

planning.

PHOTO/JEFFREY YARDIS

HRH INSURES HIGH-PROFILE LOCAL ORGANIZATIONS, INCLUDING RIVERFRONT RECAPTURE. FROM LEFT, JOE MARFUGGI, CEO AND PRESIDENT OF RIVERFRONT RECAPTURE, TALKS WITH HRH CLAIM ACCOUNT MANAGER, TED SHAFER, AND CLIENT EXECUTIVE, RON SUTEK, DURING AN ON-SITE VISIT.

The company's Hartford presence began in the 1930s, at 41 Lewis St. in historic downtown Hartford. The founders of that agency, Goodwin, Loomis & Britton, had deep roots in the community. Members of their families founded several well-known Hartford landmarks, including Goodwin Park, the Goodwin Hotel and the Loomis Chaffee School.

One of the firm's founders started an insurance program for local colleges and students, and the majority of those educational institutions remain HRH clients today. Employees of GLB still working with HRH, can recall how business has changed since the days when it was not uncommon for an account executive to bring a dozen eggs and a pound of bacon to a client's home for breakfast and a discussion of their insurance program. Over time, as the pace of business quickened, the employees of GLB changed their business practices to keep pace. They replaced typewriters with computers for insurance applications and proposals, and acquired their first facsimile machine in the mid-1980s. After outgrowing its Lewis Street location, Goodwin, Loomis & Britton relocated to State House Square, where the company became its first tenant. Today, HRH remains a major tenant and is planning a mid-2005 move within State House Square to accommodate its ongoing growth.

A major competitor of GLB's was Kenney, Webber & Lowell, located in Canton. The

two companies were both full-service agents and were close in size, with GLB's 30 employees and KWL's 40. Kenney, Webber & Lowell was well known in the Farmington Valley, with specialty expertise in insurance for fuel oil dealers, small business and personal lines.

The two companies would eventually have something else in common: both would merge into American Phoenix, the property and casualty brokerage subsidiary of Hartford-based Phoenix Home Life Mutual Insurance Co. The broker purchased Kenney, Webber & Lowell in 1982 and Goodwin, Loomis & Britton in 1995. During that period, American Phoenix was the 14th largest property and casualty insurance brokerage firm in the United States.

In the late 1990s, the success of American Phoenix raised the interest of the nation's seventh largest broker, Virginia-based Hilb, Rogal and Hamilton. The subsequent 1999 merger in Hartford of American Phoenix and publicly-traded HRH would have a great impact on the entire company just a few years later, when local Chairman Mell Vaughan and President Robert Lockhart would ascend to senior management positions at HRH headquarters. Today, these inspirational executives lead their 3,500 colleagues nationwide as CEO, and president and chief operations officer, respectively.

Growth continued for HRH's operations in Hartford in 2001, when it acquired

B. Perkins & Co., an independent firm owned by Brewster Perkins. Located in the United Way building on Laurel Street, B. Perkins was well known throughout Hartford for its work with nonprofit organizations, and for insuring high-profile sports teams and community landmarks. Founded on April 1, 1980, with three employees, B. Perkins & Co. joined HRH exactly 21 years later with 20 employees and annual revenues in excess of $3 million.

The most recent and largest merger in HRH's history was completed in July 2002 with the addition of Atlanta-based Hobbs Group, a 500-employee firm specializing in risk management and insurance services for Fortune 1,000 companies. In recognition of the significant expansion of the company's capabilities, a decision was made to rename the firm Hilb Rogal & Hobbs. The firm continues to recognize the contributions of founder David Hamilton with an annual award in his name – the David W. Hamilton Integrity Award – presented to an HRH employee nominated by fellow employees for dedicated and honorable performance.

While the names have changed since the company's beginnings in the 1930s, its focus remains on accountability to clients, passion for its business, hiring the best talent and conducting business and personal relationships with integrity. These are the four values for which HRH clients recognize the firm.

Specialist Knowledge

From Fortune 500 companies to trade associations, individuals and small businesses, HRH provides tailor-made risk management solutions based on expert advice and customized risk assessments. The firm has specialists with knowledge depth in many client industry groups, including private schools, nonprofit organizations, fuel oil distributors, manufacturing, health care and technology. Its global partner network facilitates the integration of customers' domestic and foreign risk exposures into coordinated insurance programs designed to ensure consistency across the world.

Unparalleled Service

From risk assessments to claims management, at HRH the motto is simple: "We make excellence routine." HRH develops personal relationships with clients and enjoys being a valuable part of their management teams.

HRH develops comprehensive, strate-

gic programs and services to lower the cost of doing business by controlling the factors that contribute most to risk. HRH maintains excellent relationships with the best carriers in the business, ensuring access to a large range of markets and products to serve any need. In addition, its strong relationships and significant premium volume with many insurers often results in cost savings for clients.

Community Responsibility

HRH takes seriously its responsibility to improving the communities in which its employees live and work. Its corporate partnership with Habitat for Humanity resulted in a new home for a Hartford family in September of 2003. HRH provided

the financial assistance and dedicated employees to construct this family's home throughout the summer of that year.

HRH employees also participate in the United Way's Day of Caring, Walk for the Cure and numerous other local activities supporting the community. Team HRH looks forward to competing in the Dragon Boat races, an annual event sponsored by Riverfront Recapture.

In today's wired world, most business transactions can be done by phone, e-mail or fax. While HRH is the seventh largest broker in the United States, its professionals know the value of conducting business on a local level. The insurance, employee benefits and financial planning professionals of Hilb Rogal & Hobbs strive every day to make a positive impact on the businesses and organizations they serve throughout the Hartford region and around the world.

HRH VOLUNTEERS RAISE THE FIRST WALL ON THE HOME THEY BUILT FOR THE HARTFORD AREA HABITAT FOR HUMANITY IN THE CITY'S NORTH END.

CROWN PROPERTIES INC.

Since its creation in

New York City in 1982,

Crown Properties Inc. has

consistently proven that

its prudent investment

decisions, hands-on

management style and

excellent customer service

are the tools for success

in commercial property

management.

PHOTO/MATTHEW GARDNER

THE PEACEFUL SETTING OF
CROWN PROPERTIES AT
GRIFFIN OFFICE CENTER
MAKES IT A DESIRABLE
LOCATION FOR EMPLOYEES AND
BUSINESS OWNERS ALIKE.

*I*ts mission is simple: to create real value in every property by providing sought-after amenities through innovative capitol improvements and state-of-the-art technologies without excessive costs.

Crown Properties owns approximately 3 million square feet of office space in the eastern half of the United States. With an average building size of 425,000 square feet, Crown Properties has strategically positioned its portfolio to concentrate only on Class A and B assets. With properties in major cities in New York, Connecticut, Indiana, Pennsylvania, Texas and Virginia, Crown Properties focuses on providing office space that is located in the most desirable regions possible. Its Connecticut locations, which account for approximately 25 percent of its portfolio, are prime examples.

The first, located at the heart of the Griffin Office Center, a premier 600-acre, master-planned business park that contains more than 2 million square feet of Class A office space and industrial development, is easily accessible from New York and Boston. Located approximately 10 miles north of Hartford, on the Windsor and Bloomfield town lines, the Griffin Office Center is an ideal spot for growing businesses in central Connecticut such as ALSTOM, Great American Insurance Company, and the United States Postal Service. All of the buildings in the Griffin Office Center have a view of a lake and reflecting pond and are surrounded by a jogging trail and other recreational areas, including a health club. The outdoor dining and warm, welcoming two-story atrium lobbies are typical of buildings in Crown Properties' portfolio.

The second Connecticut Crown Properties office space, located just outside of the Greater Hartford area on the shoreline town of Milford, also illustrates the firm's attention to detail and focus on providing the best possible amenities. The property boasts a 5,000-square-foot health club and a 15,000-square-foot cafeteria for employees. Tenants are also able to take advantage of the nature trails and outdoor recreational facilities surrounding the buildings. Major tenants have included Warnaco, Ann Taylor, Centex Homes and Sikorsky Aircraft.

The Crown Properties portfolio includes some of the most desirable buildings in New York City, Philadelphia, Dallas, San Antonio and Roanoke, Va. The buildings offer upgraded security control systems, on-site restaurants and caterers, drug stores, advanced heating and cooling systems, and beautiful architecture. Tenants have included KPMG, AT&T, American General, IBM, Hartford Life, Federal Express and many other national companies. The staff at Crown Properties, led by Davar Rad, knows how to turn an average property into a magnificent and sought-after Class A property and they pay close attention to markets that are on the verge of a rebound for potential growth opportunities. The management style focuses on local attention with national resources and understanding. Rad and his team are dedicated on a local level; they know what is going on at each of their buildings. Despite plans for future acquisitions, Crown Properties intends to never get so big that it loses sight of its signature commitment to each property.

DUNCASTER

Located on an 87-acre countryside campus in Bloomfield, Duncaster is one of the most respected life care communities in New England.

Duncaster residents stay active through a variety of educational and recreational programs and excursions to concerts, theaters and museums. Others enjoy fitness classes or participating in outreach projects. Whatever the pastime, Duncaster residents know that a continuum of skilled health care and assisted living services are always available within their community.

Residents embrace new experiences, personal growth and camaraderie, knowing that should they ever need skilled nursing care in the future, the services are provided for them at Duncaster at no additional cost.

Duncaster was founded 20 years ago by a group of community leaders who believed that those who live in a community have a right to govern it. It is this philosophy – "The Duncaster Difference" – that separates Duncaster from other life care communities. Duncaster residents are actively involved in how the community operates. This includes holding three seats on Duncaster's board of directors and active involvement on all of Duncaster's committees.

Living at Duncaster means security and safety paired with elegance and freedom. Residents select from comfortable studios to spacious three-bedroom apartments featuring high ceilings, large windows, generous closets, efficient storage, private balconies or patios, individually controlled heating and air conditioning, a fully equipped kitchen, and wall-to-wall carpeting.

Within Duncaster's Commons, residents gather to dine, socialize and explore new interests. The Commons includes a dining room, banking and postal services, a gift shop, state-of-the-art fitness room, library, computer room, beauty salon and barbershop, convenience market, auditorium, greenhouse and indoor gardens, activities center, and guest suites. An Olympic-size pool and a café will be added in 2005.

Executive and pastry chefs provide a fine dining experience for Duncaster residents, while a professional fitness trainer provides guidance on exercise and nutrition to maintain healthy, active lifestyles. Aging in Motion™ is a belief that wellness programs and socialization are key to healthy living, which is why Duncaster offers its residents social, fitness and cultural programs.

Duncaster's programs include lectures, group trips to the symphony, theaters, museums, sporting events and parks, a Senior Academy offering college level courses, musical presentations, art instruction, transportation for shopping, and fitness and exercise classes.

Health Care: For the Mind, Body and Soul

Good health is at the heart of Duncaster living. Residents get the care they need, when they need it. Duncaster is aligned with some of the region's best medical professionals through Hartford Hospital, including the chief of geriatric medicine who serves as the medical director. Residents build relationships with doctors, advanced practice and registered nurses, geriatricians, dentists, and physical therapists who offer services from Duncaster's Sheila Murphy Clinic and Caleb Hitchcock Health Center.

The new Caleb Hitchcock Health Center breaks the mold on how a skilled nursing and assisted living facility should look. Clusters of 12 private rooms around a shared parlor replace the traditionally long and lonely corridors of many nursing homes. Each private room is large and light-filled, with easy-access showers. Dining rooms feature cozy areas for small groups of diners, the two-story atrium "park" brings nature inside, while an outdoor flower and vegetable activity garden enables residents to enjoy nature in a secure environment.

By redefining retirement living, Duncaster is a place that welcomes involvement yet respects privacy; provides the freedom to travel, learn and grow; and offers care for the mind, body and soul.

OFS SPECIALTY PHOTONICS DIVISION

When OFS Specialty Photonics Division was founded in Avon in 1984, the fiber optics industry was in its infancy. The company's original mission was to design a new type of optical fiber that could withstand the harsh environment and conditions of use found in the mining industry.

The company discovered just such a fiber with the invention of Hard Clad Silica. It patented and trademarked HCS, which is now the industry standard for optical fibers used in rugged environments. This flagship development made OFS one of the first manufacturers of optical fibers. The development of other glass technology companies in the Connecticut River Valley and surrounding sections of northern Connecticut and south central Massachusetts would later earn the area the nickname "the fiber optic valley."

Over time, OFS evolved with changing trends in the optical fiber market and now offers a broad range of products and services, including cabling and assembling capabilities. Its latest developments are still expanding the range of applications for fiber optic technology – supercontinuum generation, highly non-linear fibers, ultra-high operating temperature fibers for use in geophysical exploration, and more.

Today, OFS Specialty Photonics Division – originally started as Ensign-Bickford Optics Co. (EBOC), a subsidiary of the Simsbury-based explosives manufacturer and most recently purchased as a going entity by Furukawa Electric of Japan – continues to deliver innovative solutions to clients as a fully integrated specialty fiber manufacturer.

Engineers at OFS develop preforms; draw and cable fibers; metalize, polish or custom-shape the ends; manufacture connectors; and provide monitoring software to keep everything running at peak performance.

OFS engineers focus their work on six key markets: telecommunications, industrial, medical, transportation, military and geophysical. In the medical field, OFS-designed optical fibers are found in lasers used in ophthalmology procedures and tattoo and hair removal, among others. Trains, commercial airplanes and other transportation methods also use OFS fibers, and the company is a key supplier to the United States military and its aircraft manufacturers.

Currently, OFS engineers are working to build glass optical fibers for use in automobiles being designed for the 2007 model year. They also are spearheading work in oil exploration, providing technology that transmits data for analyzing oil production.

OFS features an on-site, state-of-the-art assembly facility where highly skilled engineers build systems from the ground up, and they are always willing to customize the systems with features geared toward individual clients.

Its research and development resources – OFS Laboratories, a direct descendant of the world-renowned Bell Labs – are constantly working on next-generation products and making technological improvements and advancements. Using a unique research and development-to-market structure, OFS gets new technology tested, qualified and delivered to customers as quickly as possible.

Several acquisitions during the company's history have changed the firm's name over the years – after EBOC, local residents and international customers knew the company as SpecTran Specialty Optics

Co. and Lucent Specialty Fiber Technologies – but executives' commitment to the town of Avon has not wavered. Dr. Timothy F. Murray, president of the division and a repatriated Connecticut Yankee, continues the work to develop new product lines and add high-technology manufacturing jobs to the local economy. "We are exporting *products*, not *jobs*, because we focus on highly specialized, high applications engineering content niches. We are growing because of our focus on listening to the customer and seeking out critical problems for which they will pay well for a solution."

The Hartford area labor market is a part of the company's foundation, and when the time came to grow into a newer, more modern facility, executives chose to stay and build in Avon. OFS is strategically located in the heart of a region rich in engineering research talent. Recruiting from a highly qualified pool, OFS consistently hires employees who are well educated, and possess advanced technical degrees.

What's more, the work environment and quality of life in the Farmington Valley encourages them to stay.

In all, the company manufactures more than 2,000 products. Employees are guided by a mission statement that urges them to be the premier provider of specialty optical fiber solutions by understanding customers' needs and expectations.

OFS products and engineers aim to help customers solve problems, like how to: generate high output powers for less expense than solid state lasers; create an outdoor sensing system immune to lightning; and maintain hermetic seals in costly components which withstand high soldering temperatures.

As OFS celebrates its 20th anniversary this year, the original mission of creating a specific fiber for a specific set of conditions has been greatly expanded but still remains a fundamental driving force. Customers come to OFS Specialty Photonics Division with a problem and the company delivers practical, easy-to-use solutions using specialty optical fiber technology.

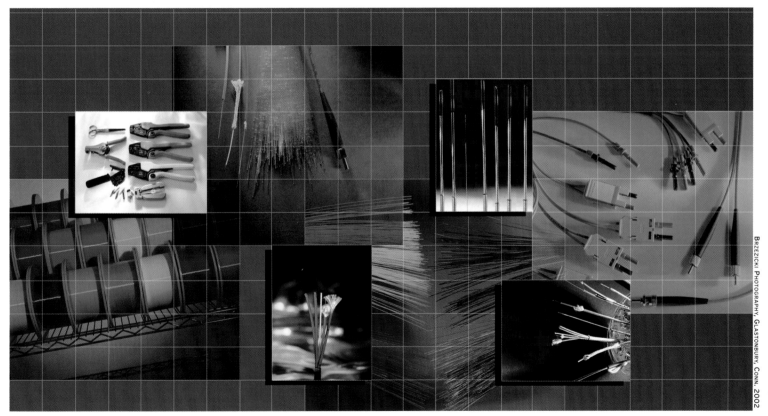

BRZEZICKI PHOTOGRAPHY, GLASTONBURY, CONN. 2002

A SAMPLING OF SOME OF THE 2,000 HIGHLY ENGINEERED PRODUCTS DESIGNED AND PRODUCED IN AVON. SPECIALTY GLASS OPTICAL FIBERS IN A VARIETY OF COLORS, SIZES AND CHEMICAL COMPOSITIONS CAN BE COATED WITH ORGANIC COMPOUNDS, METALS OR PLASTICS; REINFORCED WITH HIGH-STRENGTH YARNS OR EPOXY; CUT AND ASSEMBLED WITH VARIOUS STANDARDIZED CONNECTORS.

TOTAL FITNESS INC.

The importance of companies like Total Fitness, **a retailer of home fitness equipment, manifests itself time and again in the consumers' ever-changing needs and desires for total physical fitness.**

PHOTO/ERIC JOHNSON

NOT ONLY DO TOTAL FITNESS LOCATIONS OFFER CUSTOMERS A SHOWROOM TO VIEW A LARGE SELECTION OF EQUIPMENT, THEY ALSO ENCOURAGE CUSTOMERS TO TEST EQUIPMENT, AND ACTUALLY WORK OUT ON IT AS OFTEN AS THEY'D LIKE, BEFORE MAKING THEIR PURCHASING DECISION.

For a society often struggling with weight through diet and exercise, these desires are extremely important, and for Total Fitness, helping a client on the road to improved health through physical activity is a source of unbelievable satisfaction.

Total Fitness first established itself in 1985 in Avon. Until then, Connecticut had been lacking a distributor of home fitness equipment. Founder and CEO Jon Valles, at the age of 25, discovered while flipping through a fitness magazine in line at the grocery store, that advertisers of home fitness equipment did not distribute within the state of Connecticut. Valles, looking to fill an obvious hole in the market, set out to become the best home fitness equipment retailer in the Greater Hartford region.

Today, with a total of 11 locations and 35 employees, Total Fitness continues to provide top-of-the-line equipment, but is also committed to building lasting relationships with customers and the community. To best serve the customer, the sales team at Total Fitness must be knowledgeable about the product and the company they represent. With this information, the sales team facilitates the increasingly informed customer in

making the best decision possible for their personal needs. The company's supreme ability to retain employees has supplemented the sales team's knowledge of the company and its equipment with maturity garnered through their years of experience. The mutual relationship of trust and respect established between company and employee directly influences the relationship Total Fitness has with its customers. Without a doubt, the customer is aware of the sales team's ability to properly and professionally assist them, and the repeat customer has confirmed this time and again.

Over time, Total Fitness has seen tremendous growth within the company, and has made customer satisfaction one of its highest priorities. With stores located in White Plains, N.Y., New Hampshire and the Boston area, the company is continually looking to expand the areas it services. Recently, Total Fitness was named the exclusive seller of multiple home fitness equipment lines, a fact that speaks very highly of a company that refuses to carry anything but the best products.

Other changes occurred for the company's headquarters, including the 2001 construction of, and move to, its current location at 274 Nutmeg Road S. in South

Windsor. The move was advantageous for Total Fitness because the building was designed specifically to meet its needs. For example, its three docks, one of which is hydraulic, make deliveries, which are an essential part of their business, far more streamlined than they have ever been before.

The move was significant for the community as well. Like customer satisfaction, giving back to the community is something in which the company takes great pride. When construction of the new facility began, Valles knew there were no practice facilities to provide year round wrestling opportunities. With this in mind, construction at the new Total Fitness location incorporated a wrestling facility into the plans, ensuring that anyone and everyone interested in the sport would have a place to go. Now with an established New England team, wrestlers from all over the region have found solace in what may seem an unlikely source.

Like local wrestlers, the Griffin Foundation may have originally wondered how Total Fitness would be able to help its organization. But the wonder of using treadmills to support its cause turned to gratitude, as significant amounts of money were raised for the foundation, which helps children with cancer.

On Martin Luther King Jr. Day in 2004, Total Fitness implemented its first ever treadmill marathon. Local radio stations announced the event weeks in advance in hopes that people would sign up and take turns in the 26-mile stationary event. The day of the event proved to be a pleasant surprise for everyone involved; turnout was much larger than expected, thousands of dollars were raised, and Whole Foods donated time, food and beverages. At the end of the day, it was determined that in years to come, Total Fitness would need to bring a few more treadmills.

Ideas for charity events and ways to better serve the customer are in constant circulation at Total Fitness. One-day events, such as Total Madness in March, that provide equipment to customers at aggressively discounted prices, are at the heart of the company and how it works to better serve the buyer. Over the years, Total Fitness has had its share of "curveballs" but with a vision, strong leadership, and a sales team dedicated to working together, these challenges have been met head on. Like any challenge, these curveballs can be made easier when armed with the proper equipment. Total Fitness, aware of how daunting a task getting in shape can seem, not only provides top-of-the-line equipment, but also reminds you that the road to better health can start in the home.

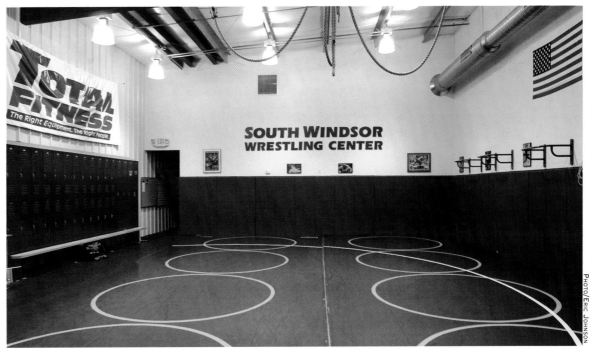

PHOTO/ERIC JOHNSON

CHILDREN FROM AS FAR AS RHODE ISLAND AND MASSACHUSETTS COME TO THE SOUTH WINDSOR WRESTLING CENTER TO TRAIN YEAR-ROUND; CURRENTLY, TWO NATIONAL CHAMPIONS ARE TRAINING AT THE CENTER. THE TOWN PROGRAM PROVIDES FIRST- THROUGH EIGHTH-GRADERS AN OPPORTUNITY TO TAKE ADVANTAGE OF THE CENTER.

MAY, BONEE & WALSH

In the business of turning achievements into stable and enduring financial positions, May, Bonee & Walsh has been serving Greater Hartford for nearly 20 years.

PHOTO/STEVE LASCHEVER

PICTURED ABOVE, FROM LEFT, ARE EDWIN H. MAY, III, CLU, CHFC, PHILIP M. BONEE, CLU, AND PATRICK R. WALSH, CIC. WITH THEIR MORE THAN 80 YEARS OF COMBINED EXPERIENCE IN INSURANCE AND FINANCIAL PLANNING, TED, PHIL AND PAT ARE HIGHLY COMPETENT PROFESSIONALS WHO HELP CLIENTS SECURE THEIR FINANCIAL FUTURES.

*I*n fact, this independent, multi-line insurance provider and financial planning firm works almost exclusively with individuals and businesses that have experienced success and want to make their money work hard for them while securing the future and avoiding unnecessary taxation.

Together, Ted May, Phil Bonee and Pat Walsh have more than 80 years of combined experience in the insurance and financial planning fields. Key to maintaining their roster of content and well-satisfied clients, they conduct an in-depth analysis of each client's current situation before suggesting, for example, the best way to set up a qualified retirement plan, purchase group or key-person insurance, fund a buy-sell agreement, or properly structure their business and personal insurance interests. May, Bonee & Walsh is steadfast in the belief that while it is the firm's responsibility to point out alternatives and all the implications of choices, final decisions always belong to the client.

In the office or out in the community, the character and commitment of May, Bonee & Walsh is well documented. Ted, Phil and Pat believe that volunteer service is a privilege. Among the many community organizations they have served are the Greater Hartford Jaycees/Buick Championship (formerly the Greater Hartford Open), the First Tee of Connecticut, the Boys and Girls Clubs of Hartford, the Children's Home of Cromwell, the Greater Hartford Easter Seals, and Northwest Catholic High School. Ted and Phil served as chairman of the Greater Hartford Open in 1983 and 1986 respectively, and Ted has served as the PGA TOUR Liaison for the GHO/Buick Championship management committee for the past 20 years. May, Bonee & Walsh supported the Jaycees as a "bridge sponsor" for the 2003 Greater Hartford Open, and has been an active supporter of the MetroHartford Alliance and the Middlesex County Chamber of Commerce.

Working as a professional 18-member team, May, Bonee & Walsh represents many of the leading insurance carriers, health plans and financial service companies and offers all lines of commercial and personal property casualty insurance, individual life insurance and investments, group insurance, and retirement plans. The firm's other professional services include personal financial planning, estate analysis, risk management and wealth management services. May, Bonee & Walsh is affiliated with National Financial Partners and its securities and investment advisory services are offered through Linsco/Private Ledger, Member NASD/SIPC.

May, Bonee & Walsh continues to provide the business community with an outstanding example of what being a great business is all about. It is a truly special business, committed to making our geographic region one of the best in the country.

STATE HOUSE SQUARE

Walk through downtown Hartford and chances are you'll find yourself on the brick plaza of State House Square. Whether you're looking for a piece of history, outdoor shopping or a place for your business to call home, State House Square has something for everybody.

*L*ocated in the heart of Hartford's financial and insurance district, State House Square is a striking, 845,000-square-foot, Class A office property that combines the appeal of a modern office building with the historic character of a venerable state capital city. It features exciting city space with two contemporary 14-story office towers that provide rich views of Hartford and sandwich a historical seven-story office building. This property continues to hold onto its history, despite the recent boom around it.

State House Square is a place where people work, shop, dine and enjoy themselves. At 800 Main St., just steps away, you'll find the Old State House, which serves as a central point of interest for tourists of every age. Guests of this restored national historic landmark, designed by renowned architect Charles Bulfinch, can tour the magnificent 1820 senate chamber, Victorian era city council room and the Colonial Revival-style supreme courtroom. Since 1796, when the Old State House was first built, business has been conducted in this square. By integrating historic and contemporary architecture, State House Square creates a sought-out retail and office environment.

With its multi-million dollar development projects, Hartford is in the midst of a renaissance and State House Square is a major player. It is located just steps away from Adriaen's Landing, a 30-acre convention, hotel, entertainment, retail and residential development project that, upon its completion, will attract hundreds of visitors daily. State House Square is accessible and convenient, located directly off two major interstates. City bus stops are located just across the street and only minutes away are Bradley International Airport, serving nearly 20 carriers, and Union Station, a hub for rail and bus transportation.

State House Square combines a central location with superb amenities like a 50,000-square-foot, state-of-the-art health club, a multi-restaurant food court, garage parking, full-service banks and ATMs, a U.S. Post Office branch and Morton's Steakhouse. The office complex also offers a state-of-the-art boardroom, tailor, shoe shine, wine shop and on-site catering service.

Combining extensive historical charm with modern-day amenities and convenience, State House Square is one of downtown Hartford's most desirable office spaces.

Statehouse Square is owned by an affiliate of Harbor Group International LLC, a diversified real estate investment company with both domestic and international holdings.

Whether visitors want to relax to lunchtime music on the Old State House lawn, delight in fresh roses at the Farmer's Market, or enjoy the convenience of a downtown fitness center and post office, State House Square is a unique and much-appreciated part of Hartford.

ADAMS & KNIGHT ADVERTISING/PR

The *Hartford Business Journal* lists Adams & Knight among the region's top 10 largest advertising agencies. It provides integrated advertising, digital marketing and public relations services to a national roster of clients.

"CREATIVE PROFESSIONALS THRIVE IN CREATIVE ENVIRONMENTS." THAT'S THE PHILOSOPHY OF BILL KNIGHT AND JILL ADAMS, AGENCY PRINCIPALS. THEY'RE PICTURED HERE IN THE AGENCY'S RETRO DINER, WHICH SERVES AS A BRAINSTORMING HAVEN AND COMPANY LUNCHROOM. THROUGHOUT THE AGENCY, YOU'LL FIND MANY MORE EXAMPLES OF CLASSIC ADVERTISING.

*I*deas that spark results. That's what they really seem to be cultivating down at Riverdale Farms in Avon – headquarters of Adams & Knight Advertising/PR.

This integrated marketing communications firm focuses on helping organizations of all kinds and various sizes target the right markets, craft the right messages, choose the right media, and deliver measurable results for their advertising and public relations campaigns.

"We understand what intense pressure today's businesses are under to show a return on their marketing investment," says principal Bill Knight. "So we work closely with our clients to achieve real, measurable results from their communication efforts."

Generating these results-sparking ideas is the agency's staff of 30 communications professionals, including marketing and media strategists, account managers, copywriters, art directors, designers, public relations practitioners, production specialists, and programmers.

These specialists are organized into matrix-managed teams to address each client's business objectives. Based on the objectives, the most appropriate specialists will serve on the client's team. The team will then recommend overall advertising strategies, and design and deliver specific communication tools to get the right messages out to the right audiences.

Much of the firm's recent work has been focused on helping clients more clearly define – and more persuasively communicate – the distinctive value their brand of products or services offers.

"In our time-starved society, a distinctive brand identity is becoming even more critical to every organization's success. If your prospects have never heard of you, they won't want to hear from you. And they'll be even less likely to associate with you, whether you're a product manufacturer, service provider, educational institution or charitable organization," says Jill Adams, the agency's president and majority owner.

To help clients crystallize their brand identities and competitive positioning, Adams & Knight often leads its clients through the agency's trademarked SparkStorm process. This interactive workshop, which often involves executives from across their clients' organizations, is designed to pinpoint the intersection between what organizations want to say – and what their prospects want to hear.

"That intersection between an organization's strengths and a client's needs is what defines the real value a brand can offer in its marketplace," adds Adams.

The agency currently works for a variety of different types of clients – from arts organizations and educational institutions to financial services providers and product manufacturers, from hospitals and health care providers to retirement living centers and nonprofit organizations.

To ensure their agency can consistently generate sound ideas for these organizations, both principals are passionate about fostering a culture that enables people to do their best thinking – and their best creating. That includes a fun work environment filled with retro advertising memorabilia, a team orientation that encourages collaboration, and an open management style that rewards suggestions for improvement.

So far, this management approach has been generating results of its own. The agency has experienced consistent growth since its founding in 1988 – and double-digit growth each year since 1998, despite difficult economic times. And the firm's work has earned creative awards from virtually all of the area's most prestigious industry associations, including the Advertising Club of Connecticut, the Connecticut Art Directors Club, the American Marketing Association, the Web Marketing Association, the Boston Bellringers Association, the New York One Show, the Communication Arts Journal, and the Public Relations Society of America.

"Most telling, though, is the fact that we've been able to build and sustain lasting client relationships," says Knight. "Our retention rate is currently more than double the industry average. In fact, we've been doing business with a few of our clients since we opened our doors in the late 80s."

The agency has also worked closely with a variety of pro-bono clients. "We truly believe Greater Hartford is an incredible place to live and work," says Adams. "So we think it's our responsibility – as well as a terrific opportunity – to get involved in projects that further strengthen our community." Over the years, the agency has donated services to Camp Courant, the Governor's Prevention Partnership, the Hartford Stage Company, the Wadsworth Atheneum, and the United Way of the Capital Area.

"The times ahead are going to be even more challenging for marketers – and more exciting for advertisers," predicts Knight.

"The lines between entertainment and advertising will continue to blur, which will give shape to new ways of getting your message across. In the future, we'll be helping clients create mini-movies for Web sites and interactive ads for TV. We'll be cutting through even more media clutter and reaching even more skeptical audiences. We'll be communicating across more cultures in less time. We'll be writing and designing for media that doesn't even exist yet."

But whatever the messages, the markets or the media, one thing's for sure: It's going to take good ideas to generate great results.

FOR THE PAST THREE YEARS, ADAMS & KNIGHT HAS EARNED MORE TOTAL AWARDS FROM THE ADVERTISING CLUB OF CONNECTICUT THAN ANY OTHER ADVERTISING AGENCY OR DESIGN FIRM IN THE STATE. IN 2004, ADAMS & KNIGHT ALSO TOOK HOME BEST IN SHOW HONORS.

THE OPEN ARCHITECTURE AT ADAMS & KNIGHT REFLECTS THE AGENCY'S COLLABORATIVE WORK ENVIRONMENT.

ROTHSTEIN & COMPANY LLC – CERTIFIED PUBLIC ACCOUNTANTS

The focus at Rothstein & Company LLC is specialized, hands-on attention, providing each client with the best advice and assistance possible.

PHOTO/HUNTER NEAL PHOTOGRAPHY LLC

For Alan M. Rothstein, a certified public accountant (CPA) and personal financial specialist (PFS) in Avon, making sure there are "no surprises" for his clients means getting to know them as people, as businesses and as families with individual concerns and issues. In fact, the only surprise a client may encounter is Rothstein himself, who may not fit the typical accountant mold, something his clientele and staff find very refreshing. His approach is personal and creative, while his sense of humor and sense of business brightens some of the haze often associated with tax season.

Before founding Rothstein & Company in 1981, Rothstein was a comptroller, accountant and auditor with regional and national CPA/investment firms, and on the weekends he was making house calls to do tax returns. These early beginnings and his hands-on approach remain a cornerstone of his business today and may be one of the reasons why many of his clients have stayed with him over the years. Even those who have left Connecticut behind can't seem to leave Rothstein, a fact of which he is very proud. With a nationwide clientele, which led to the recent opening of an office in New York City, Rothstein and his staff of eight are emphatic, "We are dedicated to providing the personal services that only a firm our size can provide."

Rothstein & Company is committed to helping small business owners, closely held businesses and higher net worth individuals. The firm serves as a business/management consultant, helping individuals strategize between personal and business tax concerns. The core services offered include general accounting, estate and business succession planning and income tax planning, and preparation. Through it all, Rothstein and his staff encourage clients to have an active role in their financial lives. This is why frequent client meetings are the norm and not the exception.

Amidst it all, Rothstein found time to serve as president of the Box Project, a national nonprofit organization that assists rural families in poverty, and he is past president of the Probus Club, a national organization dedicated to helping the mentally and physically challenged. He is also the youth advisor to a United Synagogue Youth chapter in West Hartford. Recently, Alan Rothstein was the recipient of the Distinguished Service Award by the American Institute of Certified Public Accountants' Personal Financial Planning Division.

Always looking to expand his services and provide his clients with more guidance, in 1990 Rothstein partnered with Kathy Norris and began managing Asset Strategies Inc., a financial planning and investment management firm. This affiliation has proven to be an important one for Rothstein & Company and for its growing clientele.

ALAN ROTHSTEIN, CPA, PFS AND HIS STAFF ARE COMMITTED TO HELPING SMALL BUSINESS OWNERS AND HIGH NET WORTH INDIVIDUALS DEVELOP COMPREHENSIVE TAX PLANNING STRATEGIES.

ASSET STRATEGIES INC.

Since 1990, Asset Strategies Inc., a registered investment advisor, has been successful in helping individuals and families prepare for a secure financial future.

*J*he key to the success of Asset Strategies Inc. is the ability of its principals, Kathy Norris, CFP and Alan Rothstein, CPA, PFS, to understand their clients. This understanding is much more than dollars and cents. "It's listening carefully to what each of our clients wants, feels and needs to ensure a financially successful life, and then responding appropriately," says Norris. Norris and Rothstein also prize their

financial advisors in the United States.

Operating under a strong code of professional ethics, Rothstein and Norris believe in planning first, then investing. And unlike many other financial professionals, Norris and Rothstein are fee-only financial advisors. Their firm doesn't sell any products or accept commissions of any kind. "By maintaining our independence from organizations that sell financial products, we believe that we are more focused on the clients'

PHOTO/HUNTER NEAL PHOTOGRAPHY LLC

KATHY NORRIS, CFP AND ALAN ROTHSTEIN, CPA, PFS HAVE EARNED NATIONAL REPUTATIONS FOR THEIR FEE-ONLY FINANCIAL PLANNING AND INVESTMENT MANAGEMENT SERVICES.

ability to translate difficult economic concepts and investment jargon into terms that clients easily understand and feel comfortable acting upon.

Asset Strategies has four offices nationwide. At home in Avon, Norris and Rothstein work together to help clients plan and invest for the future. As a boutique firm of six employees, Asset Strategies prides itself on its personalized services and prudent, customized investing strategies. "Alan and I enjoy our work," continues Norris. "We also know the importance of balancing risk and return. We pay attention to both growth and capital preservation, then we invest our clients' portfolios to achieve their goals with a level of risk that's comfortable for them."

Asset Strategies Inc. has earned a national reputation for both financial planning and investment management services. *Bloomberg Wealth Manager* has recognized Asset Strategies Inc. as one of the nation's top wealth management firms. *CPA Wealth Provider* named Asset Strategies Inc. as one of the country's top five financial planning firms. Also, both Norris and Rothstein were recognized in *Worth* as two of the top 250

needs and not product sales," says Rothstein.

Kathy Norris is a certified financial planner (CFP), graduated from Brown University with a BA in economics and received a MA in regional economics from the University of Pennsylvania. Norris specializes in investment management, integrating investment portfolios with corporate benefit and retirement plans, and college cost planning. Alan Rothstein is a certified public accountant and personal financial specialist (CPA, PFS). Rothstein has a BS in accounting from New York University's Stern School of Business and a MA in accounting from Western New England College. Both Norris and Rothstein are active members of NAPFA, the National Association of Personal Financial Advisors.

At Asset Strategies, Rothstein and Norris are confident that the diverse skills they bring to the company provide a strong combination that helps clients plan for their financial future. As the company witnesses the vast changes taking place in and around the Hartford area, they look forward to changing with the community and having the opportunity to better serve its residents.

REGO CORPORATION

Jose Reategui and his wife, Rosario, bought their first two buildings with their credit card in 1995. Now, their company, Rego Corporation, owns and manages nearly 500 rental units in 45 buildings throughout the city of Hartford.

ONE OF REGO REALTY'S BUILDINGS, LOCATED AT 277 BUCKINGHAM STREET IN HARTFORD.

ABOVE RIGHT, JOSE REATEGUI AND HIS WIFE, ROSARIO.

Today, Rego Corporation continues to be family-owned and operated, employing 45 people at its Webster Street headquarters. The firm provides affordable and desirable living for working families and individuals seeking a vibrant, urban lifestyle. Its straightforward mission is to "improve quality of life," which it does by acquiring and renovating existing properties and by constructing new ones.

In just under a decade, the efforts of Rego Corporation have resulted in an unprecedented increase in property values in Hartford's South End and consistent double-digit growth for the company. Today, as Hartford undergoes a major revival, developers and neighborhood associations alike seek out Rego Corporation to bring Jose Reategui's magic touch to new revitalization projects.

Rego Corporation's priority is attracting customers, associates, suppliers and investors who share the same core set of values – passion, integrity, compassion, honesty, quality and accountability. The firm is dedicated to forming meaningful partnerships with these people in order to achieve success. It holds strongly to the belief that its employees are the source of its strength. Jose Reategui, president and CEO of Rego Corporation, works hard to provide a rewarding work environment that encourages maximum professional growth and financial rewards.

Rosario Reategui oversees tenant relations through Rego Realty, the property management division of Rego Corporation. Under her direction, the company maintains its 95 percent occupancy rate by providing the highest level of customer services to its tenants. Mrs. Reategui and her staff are committed to respect and empathy when tenants' needs are in question. In the interest of making Hartford's neighborhoods safe and attractive, Rego Realty leases its apartments only to carefully screened tenants. This careful screening has created flourishing neighborhoods and has made a Rego address a desirable one.

Rego Construction, managed by Luis Reategui, oversees the rehabilitation of each newly acquired building and subsequent maintenance. And it does this successfully, by every definition of the word.

The integrity of the renovations of Rego's properties is under the care of Pilar Reategui. Ms. Reategui oversees the upkeep of each Rego building through the Property Management division, which employs internal staff to ensure the preservation of its buildings.

Rego Corporation consistently ranks in the Connecticut Inner City 10 Entrepreneurship Awards Program, a product of the state Department of Community and Economic Development and the Initiative for a Competitive City (ICIC) which recognizes Connecticut's fastest growing inner city companies. *Inc.* magazine has ranked Rego among the nation's one hundred fastest growing private inner city companies for four consecutive years.

Rego Corporation is committed to giving back to its community in every way possible. This, combined with the cultural diversity of the firm, is its self-proclaimed formula for personal and business success. Rego Corporation is a leader in reviving Hartford, building by building, neighborhood by neighborhood. As part of its mission to improve quality of life, the firm is committed to renovating clusters of buildings, and therefore neighborhoods.

Rego Corporation sets the standard for others to follow and hopes to begin moving to other inner-city areas in need of development to further pursue their passion for an improved quality of life.

SALAMANDER DESIGNS

Simple, refined lines

and functional form

are apparent in all of

Salamander Designs'

home entertainment

furniture.

PHOTO/SALAMANDER DESIGNS

THE FURNITURE IN SALAMANDER DESIGNS' SYNERGY AND ARCHETYPE LINES IS CONSTANTLY EVOLVING TO ACCOMMODATE HOME ENTERTAINMENT INNOVATIONS SUCH AS THE WIDESCREEN PLASMA TV. BECAUSE BOTH SERIES ARE MODULAR, HOMEOWNERS CAN EASILY CHANGE AND EXPAND THEIR ARRANGEMENTS FOR NEW AND UPGRADED COMPONENTS. ALSO SHOWN IS ONE OF THE COMPANY'S SEVERAL THEATER CHAIRS.

Salamander Designs was born of necessity. While still a student at Skidmore College, company President Salvatore Carrabba needed furniture for his audio system, but nothing available in the marketplace satisfied him. Using his experience in sculpture and industrial fabrication, along with borrowed tools, the Hartford native set out to invent his own furniture system – one that would grow and change with his needs.

A senior year independent study at Skidmore College that called for the creation of a sample business plan brought Salamander Designs another step closer to reality. Carrabba devised a strategy to manufacture and market the furniture system he had conceived.

Salamander Designs was launched in 1992 after Carrabba returned to Connecticut and provided pieces of his system to Hartford-area electronics stores on consignment. It was a hit, and Salamander Designs soon hired its first employees, sublet space from the Hartford branch of Goodwill Industries and began to employ Goodwill clients.

By 1996, Salamander Designs had grown considerably and relocated to its current home in Hartford's Parkville district, an inner-city neighborhood now experiencing a reawakening. Carrabba and his wife, Alessandra, who also manages the company, are pleased to be part of the area's renaissance. Many of the company's 25 employees live in Parkville within a short walk of their workplace, and Carrabba hopes to offer jobs to more community residents as Salamander Designs continues to grow.

In 1998, Carrabba unveiled his second furniture series. Called Synergy, it was designed for customers who prefer enclosed cabinets to the exposed shelving of his first line, known as Archetype. Like Archetype, Synergy allows people to create furniture that satisfies their needs at any given time but also lets them reconfigure and add on modules later.

Today, Salamander Designs' furniture is sold to high-end audio and home theater customers in more than 500 retail outlets. Its products, which also include media storage units and home theater seating, are built in Hartford with American-made components.

Salvatore Carrabba continues to value his relationship with Goodwill Industries. These days, the organization occupies space at Salamander Designs. Salamander Designs still continues to contract a portion of its labor to Goodwill clients, allowing them to develop personally and participate in society.

Carrabba is also committed to Parkville and the city of Hartford. When Fleet Bank awarded its Entrepreneurial Award and a $10,000 grant to his company, he donated a portion of the money to the Hartford chapter of Our Piece of the Pie, an organization that inspires and mentors young people, opening their minds to employment opportunities and providing options that lead to economic self-sufficiency. Each year, Salamander Designs sponsors a benefit concert called Metal Health, which brings numerous performance artists together for charitable causes.

Built in 1913, the Arbor Street building that houses Salamander Designs is historically significant, in part because the world's first pay telephone was produced there. Salvatore Carrabba is proud of the fact that Salamander Designs is now humming away in the old factory, continuing the tradition of innovation that has long prevailed in Hartford.

JOINING TECHNOLOGIES

In many ways, our society

is dependent on the

services of companies

like Joining Technologies.

As *Time* magazine wrote

of the company in 2001,

"Every product we use,

from CD players to jumbo

jets, are a collection of

parts that must be

glued, screwed or

welded together."

FROM LEFT, GARY AND MICHAEL
FRANCOEUR IN THEIR NEWEST
LABORATORY, WHICH BOASTS A NEW
4000-WATT CONTINUOUS-WAVE YAG
LASER. TOGETHER, THE REPUTABLE
BROTHER TEAM LAUNCHED THIS FIRST
GENERATION BUSINESS.

Joining Technologies offers precision welding/joining using high-energy laser and electron beam technology for the aerospace industries, medical device production and sensor manufacturing. Support services include engineering, high-production joining and laser system sales. Joining Technologies' quest to provide professional material joining solutions through knowledge, dedication and compassion has spotlighted the company as a high-performance business model in the region. It has earned prestigious awards such as the Connecticut Gold Innovation Prize from the Connecticut Quality Improvement Award Partnership for intelligent robotics/laser welding applications, and has earned certifications such as ISO 9001, 2000 and AS9100 that further enhance the firm's global exposure to the aerospace industry.

Electron Beam Welding

One of Joining Technologies' core competencies is electron beam welding (EBW). EBW is an established and essential process for the specialized joining of alloys in medical, defense and aerospace, space exploration, and energy development industries. This technology has not yet penetrated global manufacturing newcomers, which provides a competitive advantage for Joining Technologies. With fewer than a thousand EBW systems in operation in North America, Joining Technologies' services are of increasing importance. In an effort to sustain technological dominance, and as part of Joining Technologies' business strategy, the company is in constant pursuit of new technology and applications, which provide customers with the latest advancements for their products.

Laser Technology

Joining Technologies' introduction to laser beam welding began in 1996 with the TRUMPF-Profi micro-joining system used to provide value-added capability in collaboration with electron beam processes. A significant part of Joining Technologies' growth is directly related to laser technology developments like the TRUMPF-Profi welding system and the TRUMPF four-kilowatt Nd:YAG continuous-wave laser. This rare high-powered laser is currently replacing many fusing applications that have traditionally been carried out by electron beam processes. It has also allowed Joining Technologies to offer more efficient solutions to other joining alternatives. In addition to the success this system has provided to clients, forging a strong relationship with TRUMPF has also been beneficial for Joining Technologies. The affiliation has played an integral role in the growing recognition of Joining Technologies as one of the most progressive industrial laser welding research and development facilities in New England. The firm's continued diversification in laser technology has facilitated the company's growth and its success with clients.

Laser Robotics Applications

An important recent development for Joining Technologies was the integration of robotics and lasers in the fusing of complex component configurations like those found in cell phones. This has proven to be strategically beneficial for the company's advancement. Joining Technologies created an innovative method to bring work pieces to the laser for manipulation, as opposed to bringing a laser to the work pieces, as traditional methods do. This was done by using robotic automation combined with semi-automated work piece presentation. The 2001 breakthrough development has provided Joining Technologies with a versatile tool necessary for reaching into new markets that were previously unattainable. Joining Technologies is confident that its ability to pioneer applications and technological innovations will allow it to better serve a growing clientele.

Yesterday, Today, Tomorrow

It is with great satisfaction that Joining Technologies looks back at the measurable progress this 1990s start-up company has had since its younger days in a challenging economy and business climate. But for brothers and business partners Michael and Gary Francoeur, the greatest source of satisfaction is seeing their business philosophy in action. The company's progressive culture, high-performance attitude and continual improvement methodology prepare it for global competition. The momentum of success has driven the Joining Technologies team to emerge as a model of industry excellence, as evident in the implementation of progressive manufacturing systems, certification in industry standards and recognition as an award-winning company. Joining Technologies has been a centerpiece in the region as a high-performance business model and is often toured by local industry organizations curious about the company's success.

The growing team at Joining Technologies, which is more than 30 employees, is strengthened by its unity and aligned code of ethics. Its development and successes are fundamentally supported by the firm's corporate culture. Core values such as continuous self-improvement, opportunity based on merit, professional image and customer satisfaction direct the organization's daily decision-making process. "This core ideology and purpose describes our people's motivation and captures the soul of our organization," says Michael Francoeur.

Joining Technologies' laboratory-style environment encapsulates this same work ethic. The "visual factory effect" is prevalent throughout the East Granby facility as each lab displays lean enterprise scorecards and other signage. Each work cell is immaculately kept in order to accommodate the cleanest applications and processes routinely requested by customers. The company's "Excellence Rating Evaluation System" (ERES) ensures

the highly organized state of operational readiness is maintained with frequent inspections for efficiency, safety and cleanliness. It is this attention to detail and the company's dedication to the community that sets Joining Technologies apart from its competitors.

Joining Technologies is proud to work closely with organizations such as Asnuntuck Community College and the Connecticut Center for Advanced Technology, helping to expose students to the science of laser processing and material joining. The company continues to reach out through high school mentoring programs and encourages the employment of high school students interested in a career in advanced manufacturing processes.

Today, Joining Technologies is sought out for its intellectual value. It has met the

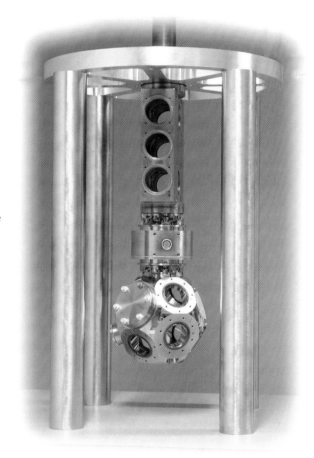

THE CORE OF A RUBIDIUM ATOMIC CLOCK FOR THE DEPARTMENT OF DEFENSE. THIS ICON IS TYPICAL OF THE HIGH-PRECISION WORK FOR WHICH JOINING TECHNOLOGIES HAS BEEN RECOGNIZED.

challenges of earning business that traditionally went to larger corporations and gaining an industry reputation for excellence. "The future holds outstanding prospects for Joining Technologies, as we reach further into future technological advances in high-energy beam applications," says Michael Francoeur. With continued collaboration with companies like TRUMPF and other Connecticut counterparts, Joining Technologies is optimistic about achieving excellence on the global playing field and here in Connecticut.

LA PERLA FINE JEWELERS

Grace. Beauty. Elegance.

With more than 25 years of

jewelry industry experience,

Bob La Perla has been

offering dazzling designs

and custom-crafted jewelry

at La Perla Fine Jewelers

in West Hartford Center

for over a decade.

PHOTO/STEVE LASCHEVER

THIS BEAUTIFUL PLAY OF COLOR INCLUDING THE INDIGO OF TANZANITE-FACETED BEADS, THE GENTLE MAUVE OF THE 9MM CHINESE FRESH WATER PEARL, AND THE RICH BLUE OF NATURAL AUSTRALIAN OPAL ALL SET INTO A 18KT YELLOW BEZEL MAKES THIS A WEARABLE PIECE OF ART.

With a name like La Perla, it almost had to be. Robert (Bob) La Perla was a 19-year-old college student looking for work when he inquired with the haberdashery at the former G. Fox and Co. department store. No positions were available, but not to be dissuaded, he vied for a sales associate spot at the fine jewelry counter at G. Fox's Waterbury location. It was there that La Perla began his career in fine jewelry. Just five months later, La Perla was promoted to department manager – the youngest in G. Fox and Co. history.

La Perla's success did not go unnoticed, and soon he was recruited by another fine jeweler. For several years, he worked and trained with some of New York's finest jewelry designers and crafters. Using his natural talent for sculpting, La Perla began creating his own designs. He eventually managed operations for 22 storefronts for a large jeweler from the Midwest. By then, he was a man with a young family; La Perla was ready for yet another challenge.

In 1992, La Perla Fine Jewelry Ltd. opened its doors at 971 Farmington Ave. in West Hartford with a mission to provide guild retail jewelry service and the sales and merchandising of rare and precious commodities, artifacts and collectibles. The venture was not without risk. The economy was uncertain, but La Perla felt that downtown areas were poised for revitalization, and strongly believed that a shift from malls to neighborhood shopping was set to begin. He could not have been more right. The block of Farmington Avenue between LaSalle Road and South Main Street, an area that La Perla had selected two years before, would become the nucleus of the upscale West Hartford Center of today.

The alluring glow of the windows of La Perla Fine Jewelers quickly attracted customers to La Perla, and Robert La Perla's reputation for personal service, coupled with the stunning displays in his showroom, soon brought the shop public acclaim. Customers have come to appreciate the style of La Perla designs – traditional in approach, contemporary in flair.

The La Perla emblem, a swan poised atop a pearl, expresses Robert La Perla's philosophy of business. The pearl symbolizes truth and longevity, the swan elegance and grace. It is La Perla's long standing belief that his success has come from truthful relationships with his customers and designing and crafting things of beauty.

Hand-selected pearls of Japanese and Chinese origin are top sellers at La Perla. Each strand is hand strung, from the simplest single strand, to La Perla's award-winning custom designs. Robert La Perla is an eight-time winner of the Connecticut

Jewelers of America affiliate design competition. He is also a national winner, with a three-strand, dyed pink pearl necklace. The necklace fastens in the front with a platinum and 18-karat yellow gold clasp that holds a 4.29-carat pear-shaped rubellite and 0.36 carat of brilliant-cut diamonds.

Robert La Perla's custom designs are a La Perla hallmark. From elegant signature pieces designed as a wardrobe cornerstone, to La Perla's exclusive Heirloom Silhouettes, La Perla takes special care to portray the spirit of the wearer.

Among the most recognizable of Robert La Perla's custom works are hundreds of La Perla Heirloom Silhouettes, meticulously cut by hand. Each diminutive charm is a moment captured in gold. The fine detail captures the charm, essence and personality of each child depicted.

Dazzling designs are masterfully created at La Perla. Two jewelry crafters from Armenia, a country with centuries-old traditions of artistic jewelry crafting, bring sketches and models to life in La Perla's West Hartford Center store.

Alongside La Perla's jewels are works of fine art from Elm Art Gallery & Studio. La Perla offers selected works from Elm Art Gallery & Studio's collection of fine paintings and contemporary sculpture of international quality, as well as the same collection of museum-grade, custom-made 23-karat gold frames.

As La Perla Fine Jewelers was entering its second decade in business, the world-renowned CowParade public art event came to West Hartford Center, bringing unprecedented numbers of visitors to Farmington Avenue. La Perla Fine Jewelers, along with 971-975 Farmington Ave. neighbors E.L. Wilde, Lyn Evans Potpourri Designs, The Toy Chest, and Andrews Ltd. Partnership, sponsored artist Natasha Sazonova's Moogic Cow, which was auctioned to benefit the Connecticut Children's Medical Center and Nutmeg Big Brothers and Big Sisters.

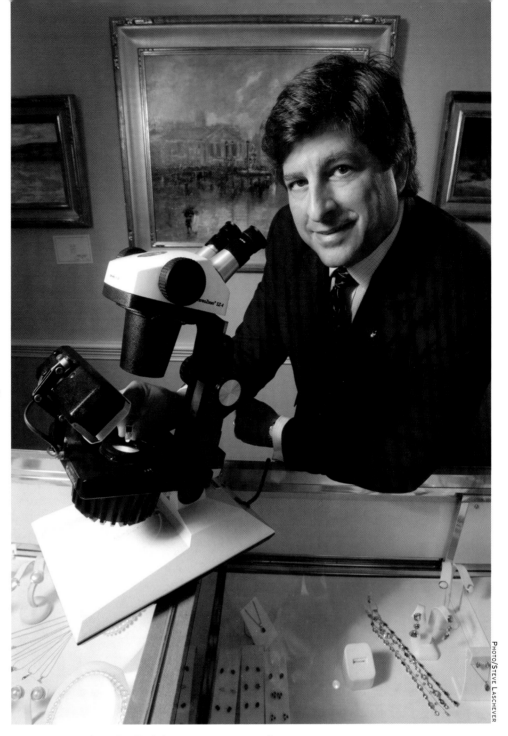

PHOTO/STEVE LASCHEVER

Robert La Perla's vision is to provide his clientele and community with quality of life and quality of merchandise. While developing his independently owned shop, Robert La Perla also immersed himself in the community, serving on the board of corporators for American School for the Deaf and on the board of directors of the West Hartford Chamber of Commerce. He has also spent six years as the president of West Hartford Center Business Association and is president of the Connecticut Retail Jewelers Association and a member of Rotary and UNICO. La Perla Fine Jewelers is also a proud sponsor of UConn Huskies football.

La Perla Fine Jewelers is a cornerstone in West Hartford Center, creating things of beauty to last for generations.

GEMS AND GEMOLOGY ARE ONLY ONE FACET OF ROBERT'S LIFE PURSUIT OF VALUE. THE BALANCE OF DESIGN, QUALITY, AND AFFORDABILITY IS WHAT SETS HIM APART FROM HIS PEERS.

HARTFORD BUSINESS JOURNAL

Entering its 13th year as Greater Hartford's premier weekly business resource, the *Hartford Business Journal* continues to serve the business community with strong news stories, innovative free-standing publications and networking events that create buzz.

hen the *Hartford Business Journal* began publishing back in 1992, central Connecticut was in the midst of a recession, and despite a number of start-up attempts, no serious business news source had successfully established itself in the region.

Aiming to provide a sophisticated market with the highest quality business reporting possible, the *Hartford Business Journal* entered and quickly dominated the market for regional business news in Greater Hartford. A few years later, in response to both advertiser and reader support, the newspaper doubled its publication schedule from every-other-week to weekly.

Since its inauguration, the *Hartford Business Journal* has been guided by its original, and very straightforward, mission statement: "We shall offer value to our readers by providing them with timely, compelling and accurate business news in an exciting and creative format. We shall be an efficient and cost-effective medium for our advertisers to reach business decision-makers."

Over the years, the dedication of every member of the *Hartford Business Journal* staff has created an environment that breeds success. The hard work and great results achieved by the team are recognized locally by readers and nationally by peers in the publishing industry.

The Alliance of Area Business Publications, the national trade organization that represents 61 regional and local business publications in the United States, Canada and Puerto Rico, has recognized the *Hartford Business Journal* with gold awards in 2003 for Best Recurring Features and in 2004 for Best Body of Work, Single Reporter. A silver award was won in 2003 for Best Explanatory Journalism. *Hartford Business Journal* reporters regularly produce timely, relevant news that business decision-makers throughout the region have come to count on – each and every week.

Advertisers also recognize the *Hartford Business Journal* as an effective tool to reach their targeted audience. The *HBJ* is one of very few regional business publications in the state to offer advertisers both an independent circulation audit and a credible readership survey, the most recent of which was completed in the third quarter of 2004.

"We're truly dedicated to being the best source available for timely, compelling and accurate business news," says Publisher Joe Zwiebel. "As our region grows," he continues, "focusing on the fundamentals of excellent journalism in an exciting format that serves both readers and advertisers will help us to do just that."

ABOVE, A SAMPLING OF ISSUES AND PUBLICATIONS PRODUCED BY THE HARTFORD BUSINESS JOURNAL.

AT RIGHT, THE STAFF OF THE HARTFORD BUSINESS JOURNAL AT THE ENTRYWAY TO THEIR OFFICES, LOCATED AT 15 LEWIS ST., HARTFORD.

PHOTO/RAMONA MANSFIELD

NEW ENGLAND COMMUNICATIONS SYSTEMS INC.

Since being founded

by four Motorola employees

in 1995, New England

Communications Systems Inc.

has quickly become southern

New England's largest

two-way radio dealer and

service provider.

PHOTO/ERIC JOHNSON

Based in Middletown, with a second office in Chicopee, Mass., NECS' experienced staff has cultivated extensive expertise in radio system installation and maintenance. The company's commitment to the customer, the marketplace and employee training, and understanding how technology solutions best fit the end user have allowed it to grow rapidly in sales volume, technical experience and system capabilities in less than a decade.

Three of its four founding partners still lead the company today – President Carolyn Windesheim, Vice President and CEO Myron Polulak, and Vice President and Secretary Gary Tallmon. Their founding mission, to be the premier Motorola supplier of wireless communications equipment in Connecticut, continues to drive them today.

Between its two locations, NECS has 44 employees: 16 service technicians, five field installers, seven sales personnel, and 16 managerial, customer service and support staff. All strive to provide their valued customers with top-quality Motorola products, systems and services in the required timeframe. They are committed to providing excellent customer service, quality workmanship, product value and total system responsibility.

From its inception, NECS hired Motorola service technicians, staff and management teams, allowing it to become a Motorola authorized service station. Coming from a Motorola background, the firm's founders and employees instilled a culture of customer service, an understanding of the marketplace, and required technical knowledge from the onset. That background knowledge has led NECS to earn Motorola's prestigious Pinnacle of Customer Excellence Award and five Motorola Pinnacle Sales Awards.

Among its growing list of customers, NECS services Connecticut Natural Gas (CNG), Foxwoods Resort Casino, Pratt & Whitney, Bristol Myers Squibb and Dominion Power.

Today, as when it was founded nine years ago, NECS generates a large percentage of its business serving clients in the public service and public safety sectors, playing a dominant role throughout central and eastern Connecticut and Western Massachusetts. The company has installed and maintains high-tech systems such as both the Connecticut and Massachusetts state police's digital simulcast voice and data networks, and various municipal simulcast systems in towns across the region.

NECS' commitment to public service extends beyond its client base, however. The company also is actively involved in area community efforts. It is a local sponsor of the Juvenile Diabetes Foundation, and in 2003 won the organization's Walk for a Cure T-shirt design contest. Walking under the team name "Two-Way Tigers – Roaring for a Cure," NECS employees participated in the 2004 Walk for a Cure in October. The company also avidly supports local police and fire unions' campaigns.

The company's commitment to excellence, both inside the workplace and out in the community, is a mainstay of its business philosophy. That strategic vision, combined with the integration of new, ever-changing wireless technologies, will keep NECS in the forefront of the two-way radio industry for years to come.

PCC TECHNOLOGY GROUP LLC

Originally established to provide support services to individuals and workplaces learning how to utilize computers, PCC Technology Group has become a premier information technology services company.

FROM LEFT, JERRY LONG, PRESIDENT AND CEO, AND JOE SINGH, PARTNER.

PHOTO/ERIC JOHNSON

The creation of PCC Technology Group had been on Jerry Long's mind for sometime, which may explain why, when laid off in 1988 from the Hartford Insurance Group, he seemed oddly at peace with the situation. Despite the news, Long remained confident. "I knew I would be in business by the time I got home." Named one of the 50 fastest-growing technology companies three years in a row by Deloitte & Touche and the Connecticut Technology Council, Long has witnessed first-hand his vision become a reality. Now, with a staff of more than 50 employees, Long, president and CEO, is extremely proud to be recognized by the industry for his company's achievements and continued growth.

PCC's successful track record of providing software solutions to global companies and local, state and federal governments has earned it a reputation as New England's leading provider of IT services. With services that include application development, e-solutions, e-government, systems integration, Web development and contract profes-

sionals staffing, PCC's talented and skilled consultants work tirelessly to provide the best service possible.

Providing clients with innovative technology solutions in support of solving business challenges and increased productivity continues to be PCC Technology Group's main objective. PCC is increasingly involved in various sectors of the business industry, including its position as a leading provider of government-centric information technology solutions. Concentrating on federal and state laws in the areas of campaign finance and centralized voter registration, PCC's election division brings impressive experience with a team of election product specialists. These specialists help clients set up and become familiar with PCC's latest software development, ElectioNet™.

Used for election management, the program is comprised of three Web-based systems: centralized voter registration, election results management and campaign finance reporting. The latter of these recently earned the Digital Government Award of Excellence. Each of the systems can be customized to meet the specific needs of varying states and clients. Electio*Net*™ is successfully running in five states, including Connecticut.

When Connecticut replaced its system with Electio*Net*™, it became the first installed site for the product, supporting two million registered voters in 169 towns for more than 600 concurrent users and 718 polling places. The product features statewide, centralized voter registration and reporting, election tallying, poll place management, as well as multiple role security. These, along with many other services, are included with the Electio*Net*™ product.

PCC Technology Group's presence in e-business and e-government solutions has made it a leading expert in the e-business arena. Today more than ever, the Web has become a lucrative channel for conducting business. According to PCC, what began as a medium for posting electronic sales brochures has become a powerful vehicle for a new business model. This evolution has inspired more and more competition, making a presence on the Internet mandatory for businesses both young and old.

The reality is that companies and products are judged largely by their Web site, and the experts at PCC are available to assist the business community with what may be unfamiliar territory. The experienced staff is knowledgeable and well versed in a wide variety of applications including customer relationship management, work flow management, supply chain management and many others.

Like other services and products provided by PCC, the global e-business solutions are customized to support business-to-business and business-to-customer relationships. The team of consultants works closely with clients to better facilitate the creation of an effective e-business solution.

One of the things Jerry Long and his partner, Joe Singh, are most proud of is their company's employment of an ever-growing staff of highly trained and skilled individuals. "Our goal has been to hire the highest-quality talent, and to have our staff continue to develop their abilities so that we can provide the best IT solutions for each customer," says Long. PCC's team has many years of comprehensive information

technology experience, particularly excelling in the integration of both hardware and software applications. The experienced consultants at PCC can help clients develop new applications as well as optimize the use of existing systems.

Whether working with small networks or large mainframes, PCC creates supportable solutions that help maximize performance, minimize downtime, and eliminate the overlapping efforts of clients' resources and personnel. The consultants at PCC work on the client's team to ensure that new systems are truly integrated and that clients receive total solutions versus just software. Every project involves tireless reporting, planning,

PHOTO/ERIC JOHNSON

FROM LEFT, DAN KATSELNIK,
LINA CUNHA AND LORI THOMPSON.

scheduling and testing for optimum quality assurance. Based on experience, PCC team members successfully utilize the myriad of technologies available in this industry to provide the kind of network unity that is vital to a successful business.

As PCC Technology Group continues to grow, Jerry Long is excited and encouraged by the changes taking place in and around the Greater Hartford area. His involvement with the MetroHartford Alliance has allowed him a firsthand glance at the various businesses in the area that are growing and developing. This involvement conjures up familiar reminders for Long, whose business grew up in the shadow of the chamber and took advantage of all it had to offer. PCC is excited for the future, and for the continued success in the services it provides, the people it employs and the relationships it develops with the community and other businesses.

Since 1996, Connecticut Children's Medical Center has been focused on one thing: making kids feel welcome while making them feel better.

Photo/Tom Hanley

CONNECTICUT CHILDREN'S MEDICAL CENTER IS THE ONLY HOSPITAL IN THE STATE EXCLUSIVELY DEVOTED TO THE CARE OF CHILDREN FOR ALL THEIR MEDICAL NEEDS. A TEACHING HOSPITAL, IT IS HOME TO THE UNIVERSITY OF CONNECTICUT SCHOOL OF MEDICINE RESIDENCY TRAINING PROGRAM IN PEDIATRICS.

At a party celebrating the fifth birthday of Connecticut Children's Medical Center in 2001, then Lt. Gov. M. Jodi Rell said, "This gleaming building was the dream of many people; a building that is medically efficient, cutting edge and kid friendly. It's a really neat gift for the kids of Connecticut."

But, equally important to improving the quality of children's health care, Rell said, "You have reduced the fright factor in kids. You make kids feel welcome before you make them feel better."

Connecticut Children's Medical Center in Hartford is the only hospital in the state exclusively devoted to the care of children and to all of their medical needs. According to the editors of *Child* magazine, it is rated one of the Top 20 Children's Hospitals in America.

The opening of CCMC in 1996 was an early signal of Hartford's emerging renaissance. Construction of the $90 million children's medical center was one of the most significant projects of the decade in Hartford and helped spawn a number of other major investments in the city's South End.

But for the children of Hartford, and beyond, Connecticut Children's Medical Center represents something more important, a hospital they can call their own.

At CCMC, everything and everyone is dedicated to the care of children. Medical equipment is child-sized, and the staff members are specialists in pediatrics. Child life specialists who are trained in child development help children prepare for, and cope with, the hospital experience.

All the inpatient rooms in the 129-bed facility are private. Each room is equipped with a bath and shower and sleeping accommodations for parents who are encouraged to room in with their child.

Parents are important members of their child's health care team at CCMC. Parents are present during all medical procedures and are even invited to accompany the child into the operating room to support the child during anesthesia. But only the children get to drive themselves to the operating room in a battery-powered Ferrari.

What is so important about a hospital just for kids?

Just ask Larry Gold, Connecticut Children's president and CEO, who has spent his entire career in children's health care: "Kids aren't little adults. Their medical needs are different, emotionally, developmentally. You know you wouldn't talk to a three-year-old the way you would talk to an eight-year-old, and you should expect your hospital to understand that too."

Gold is fond of pulling out a bag filled with blood pressure cuffs to illustrate his point. The first cuff is the standard size you would find in any doctor's office and hospital, and at CCMC, it fits around the arm of a 200-pound high school football player.

But then Gold keeps reaching into his bag, pulling out smaller and smaller cuffs, 12 different sizes in all, until he is holding one the size of a Band Aid. "This blood pressure cuff fits around the arm of a one-pound premature baby," he explains. "I have a picture in my office a father gave me. He put his wedding ring on his preemie baby's arm and it fit with lots of wiggle room.

"At Connecticut Children's Medical Center we take care of hundreds of those preemies every year, as well as kids of all shapes and sizes all the way up to that high school football player. So that's why we need 12 different sized blood pressure cuffs and people who know how to take care of kids with all of those diverse needs."

In fact, more than 150,000 kids a year visit Connecticut Children's Medical Center, from every city and town in the state. They come for outpatient primary and preventive care, emergency and trauma care, orthopedics, surgery, minimally invasive surgery, and for every pediatric subspecialty, from asthma care to urology.

Thousands of children with asthma have benefited from a new approach to care that trains doctors in the "easy breathing" asthma management protocol developed by pediatric pulmonary specialists at CCMC.

Connecticut Children's Medical Center is a national leader in developing new approaches to minimize pain and discomfort for children in the hospital. One of the country's foremost experts on pediatric pain management is a pediatrician on staff at CCMC, who provides leadership and education for clinicians in a "comfort-central" approach in all treatments and procedures for children.

Even the hospital's environment is geared to comfort. Children's art adorns the walls through a program called "Artreach" that involves children in creating art in the hospital, in schools and in the community.

Advocating for children and keeping kids healthy and safe is an equally important part of the mission of this nonprofit hospital. Connecticut Children's Medical Center programs, such as Connecticut Safe Kids, the Injury Prevention Center

and the Violence Intervention Project, work with statewide coalitions to protect children through outreach, education and legislation.

State laws mandating seat belt and car seat use for children, helmets for children riding bicycles and passenger restrictions for new teenage drivers all resulted from advocacy efforts led by Connecticut Children's Medical Center. In the past year more than 1,000 children were fitted with free bicycle helmets through the medical center's "Heroes Wear Helmets" campaign.

As part of its "Circle of Caring," Connecticut Children's Medical Center has formal affiliation agreements with nine community hospitals around the state to help improve access to pediatric specialty care. Not only do physicians from CCMC provide care to children at outpatient clinics at these hospitals, but CCMC staff also provides education and training to health care personnel at their affiliated partners to help improve the quality of care for children statewide.

The motto of Connecticut Children's Medical Center says it all: "Kids are Great! We Just Make 'em Better."

PARENTS ARE AN IMPORTANT PART OF THE CHILD'S HEALTH CARE TEAM AND MAY EVEN ACCOMPANY THEIR CHILD INTO THE OPERATING ROOM FOR ANESTHESIA, BUT ONLY THE KIDS GET TO DRIVE THESE COOL BATTERY-POWERED CARS.

PITA COMMUNICATIONS LLC

A view from the top is better, and Pita Communications is on the top of the world – or at least on the apex of the capital city.

From its 23rd-floor, purple and yellow offices at 1 State St., the creative team at the advertising and public relations agency has a stunning view of Hartford, the Connecticut River and the pristine hills beyond.

This stately setting is quite a bit different from the company's modest 1996 beginnings, when husband and wife team Paul and Kim Pita started Pita Communications in their home. Eight years later, the company has been ranked by the *Hartford Business Journal* as one of the top 25 advertising agencies in the Hartford region for three consecutive years and was named one of the leading public relations firms in the state in the *Book of Lists, Connecticut*.

that begins with intensive research and ends with powerful and strategic marketing programs, Pita Communications has been able to cultivate and evolve relationships with more than 200 companies.

As the agency's reputation for strong response, service and style grows, so does its presence in Greater Hartford. Aetna, Boy Scouts of America – Connecticut Rivers Chapter, Greater Hartford Convention & Visitors Bureau, Hartford Image Project, Duncaster, Proton Energy, Colt Gateway and UnitedHealth Group are just a few businesses that rely on Pita's creative capabilities.

In 2003, Pita Communications decided to fully commit itself to the city of Hartford by relocating its headquarters from Rocky Hill to its current downtown location.

"Hartford is in the midst of a renaissance," says Paul Pita. "And we're thrilled to be part of it. Our commitment and passion for the city is relentless. Working with the Hartford Image Project and the Greater Hartford Convention & Visitors Bureau, we're helping to drive Hartford's momentum."

No surprise that the Pita team enjoys community-based projects – they have worked hard to build their own small community. A tight-knit group, the Pita team shares a passion for their work and a desire to thrive at everything they do.

It's not all work at Pita, either. The team has participated in dragon boat races along the Connecticut River and frequents Hartford clubs and restaurants, including the Brew Ha Ha Comedy Club, and enjoys a New Britain Rock Cats or Hartford Wolf Pack game now and again.

"We have created an environment that inspires greatness," says Paul Pita. "This benefits our clients because individuals with great attitudes produce great work."

Though the scenery has changed for Pita Communications over the years, the company's commitment to excellence has never faltered. "We started our business on the premise that we see things differently and we listen more intently. Our senses live up to that challenge each and every day," says Kim Pita.

Be seen.

Be noticed.

Be heard.

INTERNET ANIMATION FROM PITACOMM.COM

Today, the 10-person company's clients range from start-ups to corporate giants, from non-profit organizations to health care and alternative energy companies. With capabilities including advertising, design, public relations, strategic consulting and interactive, Pita Communications has been recognized by both clients and industry insiders as a seamlessly integrated agency with a distinct, creative edge.

Offering its unique "InsideOut" process

Connecticut Parking Services is a Hartford-based, full-service parking management company committed to providing superior services to the central business district's residents, work force and visitors.

PRESIDENT OF CONNECTICUT PARKING SERVICES, CARLOS LOPEZ.

onnecticut Parking Services (CPS) maintains a work force of more than 20 staff members in positions ranging from management, bookkeeping and clerical to cashiers, attendants, maintenance and security. Carlos Lopez, a prominent Hartford area businessman and real estate professional, leads CPS as president and maintains a hands-on philosophy with regard to all management operations. Nelson Carvajal, a parking veteran with more than 10 years of operational experience, serves as general manager and is responsible for day-to-day operations at CPS' three downtown Hartford parking properties.

The MAT Garage

This garage is an active 975-space parking structure located on South Chapel and Trumbull streets in the center of downtown. CPS initiated management operations in March 1997, and since that time has worked diligently to improve the level of parking services and the infrastructure. In conjunction with the Hartford Parking Authority (HPA), the garage is completing a massive $5 million renovation project that included replacement of decking, installation of a traffic bearing membrane, lighting upgrades, replacement of fire safety systems, modernization of elevators, improved signage, and other aesthetic improvements. CPS has worked closely with the HPA representative, project engineers and construction contractors to keep the MAT Garage fully operational during renovations.

The Pratt/Asylum/Main Street Lot

A 210-space surface parking facility located truly in heart of the CBD, this lot serves a diverse group of patrons ranging from corporate staff members to visitors frequenting area shops and eateries. In the evening, this location is central to many of the nightspots that are attracting crowds from all of Greater Hartford. After assuming operations in 2001, CPS quickly improved all aspects of operations, including net profitability to the property's owners. Today, the firm continues to work closely with owners to improve the image of the property through a comprehensive maintenance program.

The Ann/High Street Lot

This 130-space surface lot is located on the fringe of Hartford's central business district between High and Ann streets. CPS has partnered with downtown employers to provide off-site parking for employees during a recent expansion. Since inception of services in 2001, the firm has significantly improved the lot aesthetics and provided a cost-effective parking option to downtown parkers.

The CPS Philosophy

CPS continues to offer owners a comprehensive program of services, which includes professional staffing and day-to-day management, comprehensive financial reporting, daily maintenance and project management, security services, and parking consulting. The company is a certified Set-Aside Minority Business Enterprise recognized by both the state of Connecticut and the city of Hartford.

CPS is guided by a philosophy that recognizes the importance of the customer. Location appearance, quality of personnel, customer satisfaction and meeting the goals of each facility owner are the key elements in CPS' business plan.

Both Lopez and Carvajal have significant experience, not only in parking operations, but in meeting the demanding expectations of an active service-related industry. Carlos Lopez has been integrally involved in business in the city of Hartford for nearly 30 years. He is a proven community and business leader and has been recognized many times for his contributions to numerous civic and charitable organizations. Both men are committed to making Hartford a better place to live and work, whether it's by providing convenient and reliable parking or by revitalizing neighborhoods and communities.

CAPITAL WEALTH MANAGEMENT LLC

For more than 15 years, successful professionals, business owners and executives have turned to Tom Hine, president and managing partner of Capital Wealth Management, for help managing their assets and transferring wealth.

Capital Wealth Management provides wealth management and transfer needs for successful executives, professionals and business owners, and develops strategies and solutions based on their goals.

Tom Hine founded Capital Wealth Management in 2001, fulfilling a longtime dream to operate an investment firm

PHOTO/PETER BILLARD

through which he could develop personal and lasting relationships with his clients. While working for a national brokerage firm, Hine forecasted an economy headed for decline, and sought a system that would allow him to better manage his clients' assets in a tough bear market. Hine's vision was an independent firm that would allow him to proactively manage his clients' accounts and provide a level of service that could not be offered through a large firm with a cookie-cutter approach.

Hine launched the firm in August of 2001 in Glastonbury. Many clients quickly followed him. He was transferring millions of dollars of assets from various brokerage accounts on the very day financial markets were closed by the events of Sept. 11, 2001. When the New York Stock Exchange opened a week later, Capital Wealth Management's first clients found that Hine had proactively protected their assets. It was a trial by fire. One of Capital Wealth Management's greatest achievements had occurred in its first weeks of business.

Capital Wealth Management earned the trust of its existing clients, and soon new referrals were coming to the firm. Within 18 months, Hine had added two additional staff members. Shortly thereafter, Capital Wealth Management reached an industry benchmark – $100 million in assets under management – a mark only attained by approximately 1,000 independent firms in the nation.

Hine does justice to his reputation of being proactive, providing personal attention and giving customized advice by taking in only 10 to 15 new clients each year. Working with clients to discover their dreams and aspirations, he helps map a plan that encompasses more than financial planning. Capital Wealth Management's clients are advised on all aspects of wealth and money management, investment services, asset allocation, and estate and trust planning. Tom Hine believes in the premise that each client deserves an objective wealth management team, which includes insurance professionals, a certified public accountant, an attorney and an investment advisor, each operating independently. When no member of the team is beholden to another, the result is objective advice developed in the best interest of the client.

The personal attention that is a Capital Wealth Management hallmark does not end when a client's portfolio is planned; Hine sees his clients regularly. Whether in his office or traveling for a planning session, he maintains ongoing contact to keep abreast of their life changes – anything that could affect their goals or risk profile. This regular communication with clients keeps Capital Wealth Management on task in meeting its mission: To assist its clients in making appropriate wealth management decisions, and educating and communicating regularly with its clients while providing them with exceptional service.

Capital Wealth Management's clients have access to a staff with unusually impressive credentials and a unique depth of experience.

Hine is a cum laude MBA graduate of the University of Connecticut, holds a Certified Financial Planner™ mark, as well as his certified fund specialist designation. Each member of his team holds licensure, has five to 10 years of experience in the

CAPITAL WEALTH MANAGEMENT'S FOUNDER AND MANAGING MEMBER, TOM HINE.

PHOTO/STEVE LASCHEVER

securities industry, and is degreed in the business field. The search for individuals with such depth of experience is critical to Capital Wealth Management's vision of being the most competent and caring wealth management firm in the industry.

Hine acknowledges the contributions of Chief Operations Manager Dawn Dodd, who has been with Capital Wealth Management from its inception. Dodd monitors the firm's regulatory compliance issues and oversees client programs, such as the client advisory board, quarterly client events and the company's newsletter. In addition, Dodd has been nominated for the 2003 Assistant of the Year and was named to the 2004 sales assistant advisory board at Capital Wealth Management's home office.

Tom Hine and Capital Wealth Management are firmly rooted in Glastonbury and the Greater Hartford

region. Each year, Hine mentors an up-and-coming finance student from the University of Connecticut, hires a student intern from the school and teaches finance principles to younger students through Junior Achievement. Hine even involves his clients in bettering the community through Capital Wealth Management's annual client event, which each year benefits a worthy charitable organization in the Greater Hartford area. He is also an advanced degree black belt in Shotokan Karate and has trained for more than 25 years.

Capital Wealth Management's unique approach to wealth transfer and management has helped hundreds of clients plan for the future. Tom Hine's ability to coordinate financial strategies, coupled with his commitment to personal, proactive service, has made him a trusted advisor and friend of generations of local families.

THE CAPITAL WEALTH MANAGEMENT team, FROM LEFT TO RIGHT, DAWN DODD, KHOUREE GALE-LEMAY, TIM HIGLEY, & TOM HINE.

MetroHartford Alliance:

Leadership for regional growth, a stronger capital city and business prosperity.

PHOTO/JEFF CRANDALL

THE METROHARTFORD ALLIANCE IS WORKING TO ENSURE THAT THE HARTFORD REGION COMPETES AS A PREMIER PLACE FOR ALL PEOPLE TO LIVE, WORK, PLAY AND RAISE A FAMILY.

For more than 200 years, beginning as the Hartford Chamber of Commerce and evolving into today's MetroHartford Alliance, the mission of the region's Chamber of Commerce and economic development leader, has been consistent: to ensure that the Hartford region competes as one of the country's premier places for all people to live, work, play and raise a family. Through the support of its leadership investors, strategic and municipal partners, and thousands of members at large, the Alliance focuses on key strategies and initiatives that secure a positive business climate. It also fosters growth of the region's core industries including insurance and financial services, aerospace manufacturing, high technology, health sciences, education, and arts and culture.

The Alliance is implementing a four-year plan with specific measurable goals and initiatives. These include the creation of 25,000 more jobs in the region, with 5,000 of those jobs in the insurance and financial services sector; a 12 percent increase in per capita wages; retention of 15 percent more college graduates staying in the region; and a 50 percent increase in the 18- to 34-year-old population. The accomplishment of these aggressive goals will affect tangible prosperity and a premier quality of life for all to enjoy.

Hartford's plan for its future is shaping what it is today.

In the absence of county government, the Alliance provides the unifying leadership needed to build the regional economy through recruitment and retention of businesses in the region. It works with local corporations to attract and retain young professionals, removes obstacles to growth for its small business members, provides a voice in local and regional public policy issues, and markets the region.

One of the organization's most exciting key initiatives is the region's marketing campaign, "Hartford, New England's Rising Star." The campaign is implemented by the Hartford Image Project (HIP) committee, which consists of 13 chief civic organizations. The campaign focuses on improving both perceptions and attitudes of Hartford as an outstanding place to live, work and play. In 2004, the campaign launched a national public relations initiative that has taken the region's redevelopment story outside of New England.

One of the region's oldest and enduring industries is insurance and financial services, in which the Alliance actively participates to ensure a positive business climate. The Insurance and Financial Services Cluster was formed in 2002 as part of a state/corporate initiative facilitated by the Alliance.

Today, the cluster is supported by statewide businesses, civic and government entities and educational institutions. The cluster provides the framework for cooperation and collaboration of industry leaders throughout the state. It works to create competitive advantages in business attraction, recruitment and education of a trained work force, productivity, nurtured innovation, and enhanced workplace environments.

The Alliance works with its municipalities to build their capacity to support economic development. One example is the delivery of EDPO (Education for Public Officials), an award-winning economic development curriculum presented to municipal boards and commissions. The organization also works on behalf of its municipalities to bring additional funding. In 2004, the Alliance was awarded a grant from the Federal Economic Development Administration to develop a comprehensive economic development strategy for the region. This strategy will open the door for annual federal economic development grants to assist communities in supporting new business development.

The Alliance is also focused on reducing the number of 18- to 34-year-olds leaving the area, and its work to keep more college graduates in the region is an integral piece of the redevelopment plan under way in Hartford. Along with the Alliance, many of the region's major companies have partnered to provide programs and marketing materials geared toward young professionals, such as the first-ever DVD recruitment package produced by HIP. Another project was the creation of *www.internhere.com,* an online portal that connects businesses and students through valuable internship opportunities. This work was accomplished through the collaboration with the Hartford-Springfield Economic Partnership, Connecticut Office of Workforce Competitiveness, colleges and universities throughout Connecticut and Western Massachusetts, and generous corporate support.

In its efforts to unite the entire business community, from corporate professionals to small business owners, the MetroHartford Alliance presents several events throughout the year, such as the Rising Star Breakfasts.

This, the organization's signature event, is a monthly business networking opportunity that introduces topics of importance to the business community through notable guest speakers. The Alliance also holds an annual meeting to recap the year's accomplishments as well as prepare for the upcoming year. Additionally, Business After Hours, the region's most established and well-known after work business networking event, is held monthly.

MetroHartford Alliance, in partnership with the *Hartford Business Journal,* is also proud to introduce the Business Champions

Award – Hartford Region's Fastest Growing Private Companies. This newly created award is given to the top small businesses located in the Hartford region that have achieved the largest year-over-year percentage increase in revenues.

Anticipating change and being armed with new initiatives and inventive ideas is a key factor in keeping cities and regions competitive and poised for the ever-changing world economy. For the MetroHartford Alliance, this has meant facilitating the expansion and growth of its existing industries, fostering new niche spin-offs from its core businesses, and bridging business and academia to maintain a center of excellence for its highly productive work force – the intellectual capital that continues to drive the region's business and economy. These tactics have put Hartford out front as a region on the move, a region undergoing a rebirth, a region that is New England's Rising Star.

REDUCING THE NUMBER OF 18- TO 34-YEAR-OLDS LEAVING THE AREA AND RETAINING MORE COLLEGE GRADUATES IN THE REGION IS A KEY INITIATIVE OF THE METROHARTFORD ALLIANCE.

RETAIL BRAND ALLIANCE

Claudio Del Vecchio, president and CEO of Retail Brand Alliance Inc. in Enfield, not only welcomes the challenge of a new acquisition to his portfolio, he embraces it with confidence and a strong sense of social and personal responsibility.

CLAUDIO DEL VECCHIO,
RBA GROUP PRESIDENT.

On April 1, 1950, when Charles Carples and Stan Vogel opened a 10-foot-wide store in West Hartford and hired their wives as sales associates, Casual Corner was born. Twenty years later, the U.S. Shoe Corp. purchased the family-owned retail company from Carples and Vogel, affording growth and expansion opportunities. This expansion led to diversification into special sizes – growing into a nationwide apparel chain.

In 1995, when the Del Vecchio family acquired the U.S. Shoe Corp., the purchase included the company's optical, footwear and apparel divisions. While the optical division was the inducement, the growth opportunity of the apparel division soon became apparent. Because of the highly qualified associates at the Casual Corner Group's Enfield headquarters, whom he had gotten to know personally in the 10 months that he spent evaluating the company, Claudio Del Vecchio made the decision to invest in the company.

He was very successful in doing just that and recently tackled a much bigger project: the purchase in late 2001 of Brooks Brothers. With a dedication to the fundamental values of Brooks Brothers, Del Vecchio managed to recapture the spirit and passion of the retailer's original image and create a true 21st century successor. He has succeeded in welcoming back customers who had not visited Brooks Brothers in recent years. The original mission of Brooks Brothers, founded in 1818, focused on selling only the finest, quality-crafted merchandise. Del Vecchio feels that Brooks Brothers, which recently celebrated its 185th anniversary, embodies what his company currently strives to achieve in each of its divisions: the combination of classic styling with outstanding quality and value. The acquisition was a perfect opportunity and a perfect fit.

In 2001, Del Vecchio also purchased Adrienne Vittadini, a name known for elegance and sophistication in knitwear, and Carolee Designs, a renowned and respected leader in the fashion jewelry and accessories industry. With the addition of these luxury retailers, he renamed the company Retail Brand Alliance and embarked on a mission to bring fashion from the New York runways to the streets of Connecticut and nationwide in a way that was tailored specifically to fit each demographic of the firm's broad customer base.

In the majority of Del Vecchio's recent business deals, one theme emerges: the companies all seem to have an apparent loss of connection with their customers. Del Vecchio's perception of the retail world is that customer-driven service is not what it used to be or the way it should be and he prides himself on doing things differently. Associates at Retail Brand Alliance are acutely focused on customers' needs and recognize that learning about their customer and providing fashionable, high-quality clothing at a value is what it takes to create a successful business. Del Vecchio has repeatedly proven that this guiding principle works, with the successful acquisition and turnaround of first Casual Corner Group, and then of Adrienne Vittadini, Carolee Designs and Brooks Brothers.

Today, Retail Brand Alliance is steadily growing and improving. It is the third largest specialty retailer in the country, behind only the Limited Inc. and Gap Inc. In 2000, the

© 2004 DANIEL MINICUCCI, RETAIL BRAND ALLIANCE

company's national headquarters celebrated its 50th anniversary in Enfield where the firm employs 700 of its 15,000 employees. Unlike many retailers, Retail Brand Alliance uses state-of-the-art distribution techniques, and products for each of its brands come from the distribution centers located just minutes away from the company's headquarters.

Retail Brand Alliance is committed to constant social improvement. Through the organization's efforts, $1.4 million has been raised in previous years for the Breast Cancer Research Foundation. Annually, RBA also strives to raise money to help eradicate colorectal cancer, and is involved locally with the MetroHartford Alliance, Make a Wish Foundation, Dress for Success and other local nonprofits. Del Vecchio has also been recognized personally for his support of the Helen Keller Foundation.

In addition to a strong dedication to social responsibility, Retail Brand Alliance is equally committed to identifying and responding to the specific needs of each of its customer groups, especially during times of wavering customer confidence. Del Vecchio believes the most valuable relationship he has is that with his customers. Building these relationships through the years, knowing its customers, and responding to their needs is how Retail Brand Alliance builds and sustains the longevity of its brands. Sherry Maysonave, communication-image consultant and best-selling author of Casual Power, says that "…the team at Casual Corner Group is committed to helping women address the challenge of selecting clothes that will power them up in their work environment." Del Vecchio and the staff at Retail Brand Alliance is dedicated to providing the resources for their customers to find the clothing that truly represents their style through an enjoyable shopping experience supported by a high level of customer service and fine quality

ADRIENNE VITTADINI

CAROLEE

BROOKS BROTHERS

CASUAL CORNER GROUP

merchandise at a great value.

Growth through acquisition positions Retail Brand Alliance as a thriving organization that gains momentum every day. Del Vecchio, who attributes his success to a mix of luck, opportunity and a highly qualified work force, is a man of respect and responsibility. Despite the challenges and uncertainty, the Retail Brand Alliance mission remains strong. The firm is committed to be a premier retail group with a portfolio of highly specialized fashion companies, each with its own distinct brand positioning and consumer identity.

**Some of this content was paraphrased from an article that appeared in the Oct. 13, 2003, issue of the *Hartford Business Journal*.

THE BRANDS OF RETAIL BRAND ALLIANCE.

THE CONNECTICUT CENTER FOR ADVANCED TECHNOLOGY

PHOTO/STEVE LASCHEVER

"The Connecticut Center for Advanced Technology will emerge as a means to ensure vigorous economic growth for the state and region as we continue to establish ourselves as a leader in the fields of science, technology and education."

– John B. Larson, Congressman

FROM LEFT, GUY HATCH AND KARL PREWO AT THE PROPOSED SITE FOR THE TECHNOLOGY PARK AT RENTSCHLER FIELD.

As a leader in industrial and scientific innovations, Connecticut has a distinguished history that spans agricultural machinery, firearms, and precision manufacturing through the development of helicopters and gas turbine engines. New critical technologies, including fuel cells, laser applications, nanotechnology, biomedical devices, sustainable energy and next-generation manufacturing, are currently emerging and enhancing existing regional strengths. Connecticut's historically innovative and entrepreneurial spirit, global and multicultural connectivity, and agile and adaptive work force provide the impetus for a future robust state economy.

Created in 2002, the Connecticut Center for Advanced Technology (CCAT) strives to enhance the economic competitiveness of the capital region through "Innovation–Education–Business Incubation–Collaboration."

Since its inception, CCAT has ambitiously worked to integrate industry, government and academia – a collaboration that is necessary to further the region's development. These collaborative efforts serve to enhance the capabilities of current and emerging industries, fostering innovation, entrepreneurship and new business creation.

It is CCAT's intention to expand its current presence and to promote the creation of a technology park at Rentschler Field in East Hartford that will concentrate a critical mass of technology in the region. This technology park will serve as CCAT's core, housing its three main initiatives: the National Center for Aerospace Leadership, the Connecticut Regional Innovation Center and the Center for Innovation and Enterprise Education. Bringing together this critical mass of technology, CCAT expects a transformational change to take place in the region – one that capitalizes on the significant strengths that exist in this area.

Technology

The creation of a National Center for Aerospace Leadership (NCAL) will support continued U.S. leadership in aerospace research and development, and strengthen the U.S.-based manufacturing supply chain. The NCAL will bring the most current and appropriate technologies to the region, while simultaneously transferring this valuable information to the region's enterprises.

Connecticut is currently home to several of the world's leaders in laser system development. CCAT has established a Laser Applications Laboratory to maintain this leadership. This laboratory was developed with the recognition of the importance of lasers for the next generation of manufacturing processes and the potential that lies in process technologies for other industrial sectors. These efforts will promote the development and implementation of lasers in the fields of manufacturing and materials technology; medical and life science applications; measurement and diagnostics; and sensors. The laboratory will contain laser-based equipment and a professional staff, as well as provide a place for colleges and universities to undertake projects requiring specialized equipment and expertise. The lab facilities will be open to companies, organizations and academic institutions wishing to collaborate on these and other topics.

CCAT's sustainable energy programs focus on solutions that lower energy costs and increase long-term energy reliability through continued partnerships with industry, government and academia – a coalition that has proven powerful and successful. CCAT will promote innovative energy and infrastructure planning, including hydrogen and fuel cell advancement, energy security, geographic profiling, and renewable energy technologies. CCAT will build upon the significant leadership of Connecticut companies, which currently conduct research and develop products in the exciting areas of fuel cells, hydrogen and other forms of sustainable energy.

Innovation

The Connecticut Regional Innovation Center serves as a business incubator to assist both start-up enterprises and established companies. The goal of the center is to foster innovation, entrepreneurship and new business creation. The Innovation Center will be a source for collaboration and an opportunity for businesses and organizations to network.

In support of new company creation and entrepreneurs, the state of Connecticut recently designated CCAT as the state's Small Business Innovation Research (SBIR) service agency. Establishing a focal point for SBIR support will assist small firms with the capability, capacity and interest in developing new products or processes. The Innovation Center is also part of Connecticut's Incubator Network, which builds reciprocal arrangements between regional incubators for space and services, in order to access markets and make links to other resources and networks.

Education

During the past two years CCAT's Center for Innovation and Enterprise Education has collaborated with several academic and public institutions in the region. The Education Center has created and successfully implemented the Science-ACT program for middle school students, a program that is currently expanding statewide. This program engages seventh- and eighth-grade students in Web-based, collaborative learning and analysis, and seeks to enhance interdisciplinary science, math, technology and communication skills. Students partici-

pating in this program address real-world problems that affect our global society.

The Education Center has also established the Community Science program that features after-school and evening programs encouraging students and adults to explore careers in science and technology. These programs advance scientific literacy, increase life-long appreciation of the role of technology in our culture and provide individuals with ongoing, career-enhancing educational opportunities. In addition, Connecticut's community colleges, teamed with CCAT, have been awarded a National Science Foundation program to create a Regional Educational Center for Next

PHOTO/STEVE LASCHEVER

Generation Manufacturing, including the development of a curriculum in advanced manufacturing with both a technology and industry focus.

CCAT anticipates significant growth in the coming years, strengthening technology-led economic competitiveness for the Hartford region and creating new, high-value jobs. The bold thinking and daring actions of CCAT, in partnership with industry, government, and academia, will ensure that the region's industrial and academic resources are effectively developed and deployed to support our nation's critical strengths in defense and global economic competitiveness.

THE CCAT TEAM:

FROM LEFT, FRONT TO BACK

LESLIE FRANCIONE, KARL PREWO,

GUY HATCH, BILL SECORD,

DEB SANTY, JOEL RINEBOLD,

CHRISTI HALLSTROM, PAUL ARESTA,

STEVE ANDRADE, ANTHONY DENNIS,

KEYIA BANKS, STEVE WEINBERG,

JOE KING.

SMARTPOWER

Clean energy – energy from wind, solar, hydro and other clean, renewable sources – once seemed like a faraway, futuristic idea. SmartPower is ensuring that in Connecticut today, it's real, it's here, and it's working.

WIND TURBINES CREATE CLEAN, RENEWABLE ENERGY – ENERGY THAT SMARTPOWER IS PROVING IS REAL, HERE AND WORKING IN CONNECTICUT.

SmartPower's nonprofit marketing campaign is dedicated to promoting clean, renewable energy for our homes, businesses, communities and schools. As such, Connecticut today is becoming a true leader in promoting clean air, healthy communities and energy independence all through the use of clean, renewable energy.

Connecticut has historically relied heavily on coal, oil and natural gas for its energy needs. These fossil fuels, while successfully powering the nation, the world and even the global economy over the past century, will eventually become too expensive and too environmentally damaging to our way of life.

For too long the country has lived with fossil fuels because many believed they were simply a "necessary evil." With no other reliable and strong energy source to take their place, the United States continued to use coal and oil to heat its homes, power its businesses and live fully in today's society.

With today's technology and new innovations in harnessing clean energy however, solar, wind, hydro and other clean energy sources are now as reliable and as powerful as coal, oil and natural gas. And better still, clean energy won't harm the environment, it isn't hazardous to our health, and it allows the U.S. to become increasingly energy independent. And the best part is that it will never run out.

Unfortunately, people have viewed clean energy as an unfulfilled promise from the 1970s, an idea that is more fantasy than reality. Over the past 30 years, supporters of clean energy have allowed it to become marginalized. Worse, the clean energy industry as a whole has allowed clean energy to be seen as a weak product, as something that cannot be relied upon to power all our energy needs. As a result, people don't think of clean energy as a practical source to warm their homes, power their computers or brighten the lights of their cities.

And yet, that couldn't be further from the truth. Today, the United States has enough clean energy to power every home in 11 states, every hospital in the country or even every factory in New York, New Jersey, Pennsylvania, Massachusetts, Connecticut and Rhode Island. The clean energy the country is already making can power every computer in America.

The challenge therefore is to explain to people that clean energy today is real, it's here and it's working. SmartPower's mission is to demonstrate that the unfulfilled promise of the 1970s has suddenly become a very strong and available replacement for the polluting, harmful and expensive fossil fuels. Where people have historically thought of fossil fuels as a "necessary evil," SmartPower's job now is to explain that fossil fuels are no longer "necessary."

Since 2002, SmartPower has worked across the state to convince citizens that clean energy is more real and more powerful than they ever knew. Today, SmartPower is calling upon all Connecticut residents to purchase clean energy for their homes and small businesses. Through the state's imminent Alternative Transitional Standard Offer (ATSO), all Connecticut residents will be able to choose clean energy for their energy needs. When the program is in place, Connecticut residents will be able to "check a box" and start buying clean energy. It's that simple. Residents can choose clean energy without making any changes to their

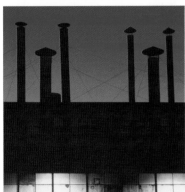  

energy consumption or their daily routine. Their lights will still go on, their air conditioning will still work and their energy needs will continue to be met. In short, absolutely nothing will change, except that they will be doing their part to help ensure clean air, a healthy community and true energy independence.

SmartPower has already seen dramatic success here in Connecticut. Working with its collaborative partners, the Clean Water Fund, Environment Northeast, and the Interreligious Eco-Justice Network, SmartPower encouraged the city of New Haven to commit to the "20 percent by 2010" campaign. In January 2004, Mayor John DeStefano of New Haven announced that the city would purchase 20 percent of its electricity from clean energy sources by the year 2010.

More recently, Connecticut provided unprecedented leadership when the governor issued an executive order calling for the state of Connecticut to buy 20 percent of its electricity from clean energy sources by the year 2010. Furthermore, the percentage of clean energy Connecticut will purchase will increase to 50 percent in 2020, and an astounding 100 percent by 2050.

All in all, within a short 12 months SmartPower helped to create more than 100 GWH (gigawatt hours) of clean energy here in Connecticut. Replacing fossil fuels with this much clean energy will result in a decrease of 160 million pounds of carbon dioxide emissions by 2010, and 420 million pounds by 2020. That's the equivalent of 45,455 passenger cars being removed from the roads for one year!

As SmartPower continues to work across the state it will redouble its efforts to call upon all Connecticut towns and cities to commit to the SmartPower "20 percent by 2010" campaign. They will call upon all Connecticut businesses, colleges, universities and faith communities to join in, proving to the nation and the world that clean energy is indeed real, it's here and it's working!

TODAY, HOMES ACROSS CONNECTICUT ARE POWERED BY CLEAN, RENEWABLE ENERGY. BY PURCHASING CLEAN ENERGY THESE HOMES ARE HELPING TO PROMOTE CLEAN AIR, HEALTHY COMMUNITIES AND ENERGY INDEPENDENCE. TODAY CLEAN ENERGY IS AS STRONG AND RELIABLE AS TRADITIONAL FOSSIL FUELS.

STEVE LASCHEVER

PHOTOGRAPHERS

STEVE LASCHEVER has worked as a freelance photographer in the Greater Hartford area since 1981. He employs an array of photographic styles, and specializes in commercial photography, annual reports, interior/architectural photography, as well as photojournalism. Throughout his career, Steve has produced numerous well-acclaimed still-image videos. Steve has served as a contributing photographer to the *Hartford Business Journal* for more than six years. He lives in West Hartford with his wife, Christine.

After 30 fun-filled years traveling the globe for corporate clients, photographing their annual reports and advertising campaigns, **JACK MCCONNELL** concedes that one of his favorite subjects still is Connecticut. For 22 of those years, he photographed in almost every Connecticut town, finding distinctive scenes for the covers of the SNET telephone directories; and for about that long, he's shot scenics and activities for the Department of Tourism and regional tourism districts. Currently, he's working on a long-range project, shooting New England stone walls, helping to address preservation issues related to this icon at risk. Jack's work can be seen at *www.stonewalljack.com, www.mcconnellpix.com,* and *www.sevenknotsgallery.com.*

He works out of his studio, McConnell & McNamara, in Wethersfield, where he maintains a library of 200,000 stock photos of New England and Connecticut.

JOHN MULDOON specializes in people, editorial, corporate, advertising, and stock photography. He is based in Connecticut and his work has appeared in the Artists of Connecticut calendars, Connecticut's annual vacation guides and the Artists of Connecticut poster series. Muldoon, who has exhibited at Hartford's Real Art Ways gallery, also was named one of the top 100 photographers in the Golden Light Awards, Maine Photographic Workshops. He is currently working on a photographic book project entitled, "People and their Passion." His work can be seen at *www.muldoonphoto.com.*

LEONARD HELLERMAN has been taking photographs for more than 50 years. His work is on permanent exhibition at the University of Connecticut Health Center Cancer Clinic, the Hartford Hospital Clinic in Windsor, and the Caring Connection in Windsor. He has photographed projects for the Connecticut Environmental Protection Agency, as well as the Town of Windsor's quarterly calendar publication. He is a member of the Connecticut Academy of Fine Arts and lectures for local camera clubs.

HUNTER NEAL is a commercial photographer based out of Simsbury, Connecticut. He is a graduate of the Rochester Institute of Technology, and headed the photo department at The Hartford for eight years. He has been an independent freelancer for more than 10 years, and his photography has received awards from the Connecticut Art Directors Club and several different organizations which conduct juried competitions for print and advertising output, particularly in the financial services arena. His work can be seen at *www.hunternealphotography.com.*

LANNY NAGLER is an award winning Hartford, Connecticut-based commercial photographer, specializing in corporate/industrial, advertising and travel photography. Over the past 27 years, his work has appeared in magazines, annual reports, ads and brochures for Fortune 500 clients in this country and throughout the world. He is currently president of the Connecticut chapter of the American Society of Media Photographers and is on the board of the Connecticut Art Directors Club. His work can be seen at *www.lannynagler.com.*

Finding his inspiration in everyday scenes, Hartford, Connecticut-based **PAUL CONEE** began shooting in 1977. His friend, and master photographer, Charles Vendetti, played the key role in the development of Paul's ability, graciously providing Paul with an education in photography. This knowledge enabled Paul to create, via the camera, the types of images he wanted to see.

People began to notice Paul's work, and on occasion, would acquire some of his works, or ask him to shoot various subjects on spec. Gradually, Paul began photographing to accommodate the interests and needs of others. Recently, he has been photographing for the Greater Hartford Arts Council and The Artist's Collective, along with various commercial interests.

A native of Hartford, **KAREN O'MAXFIELD** has been a photographer for more than 20 years. Her work has been published in the *New York Times, The London Sunday Independent,* as well as in several books and magazines. Specializing in architectural and abstract photography, her images have been exhibited throughout the Northeast and purchased by corporate and private collectors. She resides in Hartford, where she operates Studio O'Maxfield, a graphic design and fine art stock photography agency. Her work can be seen at *www.omaxfield.com.*

JERRY MARGOLIS is a Hartford area native and businessman whose avocation for the past 30 years has been photography. As the photographer for the Hartford Civic Center since 1981, the CTnow.com Meadows Music Centre since its opening in 1996 and, most recently, the Careerbuilder.com Oakdale Theater, Jerry has captured thousands of images at various concerts, and sporting and special events. He also has a longstanding relationship with UConn athletics in an unofficial capacity for the men's and women's basketball team for more than 25 years. His work can be seen at these respective venues, as well as at Coachs' Sports Bar & Grill and in *Hartford Magazine.*

Other photographers featured in Hartford: New England's Rising Star are: **NICK LACY, VINCENT SALVATORE, CARMINE FILLORAMO, TODD MEAGHER, LYNN MIKA, T. CHARLES ERICKSON, PAUL KOLNIK, THOMAS GIROIR, WAYNE DOMBKOWSKI, PETER GLASS, DEREK DUDEK, CHRIS RUTSCH, LUIS VALENTIN, RUSSELL FIELD, JENNIFER LESTER, ALLEN PHILLIPS** and **STEPHEN GIARRATANA.**

JACK McCONNELL

Index